The Woman Hater by Francis Beaumont & John Fletcher

The English dramatists Francis Beaumont and John Fletcher, collaborated in their writing during the reign of James I of England (James VI of Scotland, 1567–1625; in England he reigned from 1603).

Beaumont & Fletcher began to collaborate as writers soon after they met. After notable failures of their solo works their first joint effort, Philaster, was a success and tragicomedy was the genre they explored and built upon. There would be many further successes to follow.

There is an account that at the time the two men shared everything. They lived together in a house on the Bankside in Southwark, "they also lived together in Bankside, sharing clothes and having one wench in the house between them." Or as another account puts it "sharing everything in the closest intimacy."

Whatever the truth of this they were now recognised as perhaps the best writing team of their generation, so much so, that their joint names was applied to all the works in which either, or both, had a pen including those with Philip Massinger, James Shirley and Nathan Field.

The first Beaumont and Fletcher folio of 1647 contained 35 plays; 53 plays were included in the second folio in 1679. Other works bring the total plays in the canon to about 55. However there appears here to have been some duplicity on the account of the publishers who seemed to attribute so many to the team. It is now thought that the work between solely by Beaumont and Fletcher amounts to approximately 15 plays, though of course further works by them were re-worked by others and the originals lost.

After Beaumont's early death in 1616 Fletcher continued to write and, at his height was, by many standards, the equal of Shakespeare in popularity until his own death in 1625.

Index of Contents

PROLOGUE

Gentlemen, Inductions are out of date, and a Prologue in Verse, is as stale as a black Velvet Cloak, and a Bay Garland: therefore you shall have it plain Prose, thus: If there be any amongst you, that come to hear lascivious Scenes, let them depart: for I do pronounce this, to the utter discomfort of all twopenny Gallery men, you shall have no bawdery in it: or if there be any lurking amongst you in corners, with Table-books, who have some hope to find fit matter to feed his malice on, let them claspe them up, and slink away, or stay and be converted. For he that made this Play, means to please Auditors so, as he may be an Auditor himself hereafter, and not purchase them with the dear losse of his eares: I dare not call it Comedy or Tragedy; 'tis perfectly neither: A Play it is, which was meant to make you laugh, how it will please you, is not written in my Part: for though you should like it to day, perhaps your selves know not how you should digest it to morrow: Some things in it you may meet with, which are out of the common road: a Duke there is, and the Scæne lies in Italy, as those two things lightly we never miss. But you shall not find in it the ordinary and over-worn Trade of jesting at Lords and Courtiers, and Citizens, without taxation of any particular or new vice by them found out, but at the persons of them; such, he, that made this, thinks vile, and for his own part vows; That he did never think, but that a Lord born might be a wise man, and a Courtier an honest man.

PROLOGUE (At the Revival)

Ladies, take't as a secret in your ear,
Instead of homage, and kind welcome here,
I heartily could wish you all were gone;
For if you stay, 'good faith, we are undone.
Alas! you now expect the usual ways
Of our address, which is your sex's praise
But we to-night, unluckily, must speak
Such things will make your lovers' heart-strings break,
Be-lie your virtues, and your beauties stain,
With words, contrived long since, in your disdain,
'Tis strange you stir not yet; not all this while
Lift up your fans to hide a scornful smile;
Whisper, or jog your lords to steal away,
So leave us to act, unto ourselves, our play:
Then sure, there may be hope, you can subdue
Your patience to endure an act or two;
Nay more, when you are told our poet's rage

Pursues but one example, which that age
Wherein he lived produced; and we rely
Not on the truth, but the variety.
His Muse believed not what she then did write;
Her wings were wont to make a nobler flight
Soar'd high, and to the stars your sex did raise:
For which, full twenty years he wore the bays.
'Twas he reduced Evadne from her scorn,
And taught the sad Aspatia how to mourn;
Gave Arethusa's love a glad relief;
And made Panthea elegant in grief.
If those great trophies of his noble muse
Cannot one humour 'gainst your sex excuse,
Which we present to-night, you'll find a way
How to make good the libel in our play:
So you are crual to yourselves; whilst he
(Safe in the fame of his integrity)
Will be a prophet, not a poet thought,
And this fine web last long, though loosely wrought.

ACTUS PRIMA

SCÆNA PRIMA

Enter **DUKE of MILAN**, **ARRIGO**, **LUCIO**, and two **COURTIERS**.

DUKE
Tis now the sweetest time for sleep, the night is scarce spent; Arrigo, what's a clock?

ARRIGO
Past four.

DUKE
Is it so much, and yet the morn not up?
See yonder where the shamefac'd Maiden comes
Into our sight, how gently doth she slide,
Hiding her chaste cheeks, like a modest Bride,
With a red veil of blushes; as is she,
Even such all modest virtuous Women be.
Why thinks your Lordship I am up so soon?

LUCIO
About some weighty State plot.

DUKE
And what thinks your knighthood of it?

ARRIGO

I do think to cure some strange corruptions in the
Common-wealth.

DUKE

Y'are well conceited of your selves to think
I chuse you out to bear me company
In such affairs and business of state:
For am not I a pattern for all Princes,
That break my soft sleep for my subjects good?
Am I not careful? very provident?

LUCIO

Your Grace is careful.

ARRIGO

Very provident.

DUKE

Nay, knew you how my serious working plots,
Concern the whole Estates of all my subjects,
I, and their lives; then Lucio thou wouldst swear,
I were a loving Prince.

LUCIO

I think your Grace intends to walk the publick
streets disguis'd, to see the streets disorders.

DUKE

It is not so.

ARRIGO

You secretly will cross some other states, that do conspire against you.

DUKE

Weightier far:
You are my friends, and you shall have the cause;
I break my sleeps thus soon to see a wench.

LUCIO

Y'are wond'rous careful for your subjects good.

ARRIGO

You are a very loving Prince indeed.

DUKE

This care I take for them, when their dull eyes,

Are clos'd with heavy slumbers.

ARRIGO
Then you rise to see your wenches?

LUCIO
What Milan beauty hath the power, to charme her
Sovereign eyes, and break his sleeps?

DUKE
Sister to Count Valore, she's a Maid
Would make a Prince forget his throne, and state,
And lowly kneel to her: the general fate
Of all mortality, is hers to give;
As she disposeth, so we die and live.

LUCIO
My Lord, the day grows clear, the Court will rise.

DUKE
We stay too long, is the Umbranoes head as we commanded, sent to the sad Gondarino, our General?

ARRIGO
'Tis sent.

DUKE
But stay, where shines that light?

ARRIGO
'Tis in the chamber of Lazarello.

DUKE
Lazarillo? what is he?

ARRIGO
A Courtier my Lord, and one that I wonder your Grace knows not: for he hath followed your Court, and your last predecessors, from place to place, any time this seven yeare, as faithfully as your Spits and your Dripping-pans have done, and almost as greasily.

DUKE
Oh we know him, as we have heard, he keeps a Kalender of all the famous dishes of meat, that have been in the Court, ever since our great Grandfathers time; and when he can thrust in at no Table, he makes his meat of that.

LUCIO
The very same my Lord.

DUKE

A Courtier call'st thou him?
Believe me Lucio, there be many such
About our Court, respected, as they think,
Even by our self; with thee I will be plain:

We Princes do use, to preferre many for nothing, and to take particular and free knowledge, almost in the nature of acquaintance of many; whom we do use only for our pleasures, and do give largely to numbers; more out of policy to be thought liberal, and by that means to make the people strive to deserve our Love; than to reward any particular desert of theirs, to whom we give: and do suffer our selves to hear flatterers, more for recreation
Than for love of it, though we seldom hate it:
And yet we know all these, and when we please,
Can touch the wheel, and turn their names about.

LUCIO
I wonder they that know their states so well, should fancy such base slaves.

DUKE
Thou wond'rest Lucio,
Dost not thou think, if thou wert Duke of Milan,
Thou should'st be flattered?

LUCIO
I know my Lord, I would not.

DUKE
Why so, I thought till I was Duke, I thought I should have left me no more flatterers, than there are now Plain-dealers; and yet for all this my resolution, I am most palpably flattered: the poor man may loath covetousness and flattery, but fortune will alter the mind when the wind turns: there may be well a little conflict, but it will drive the billows before it.

Arrigo it grows late, for see, fair Thetis hath undone the barrs
To Phebus team; and his unrival'd light,
Hath chas'd the mornings modest blush away:
Now must we to our love, bright Paphian Queen;
Thou Cytherean goddess, that delights
In stirring glances, and art still thy self,
More toying than thy team of Sparrows be;
Thou laughing Errecina, oh inspire
Her heart with love, or lessen my desire.

[Exeunt.

SCÆNA SECUNDA

Enter **LAZARELLO** and his **BOY**.

LAZARELLO

Go run, search, pry in every nook and angle of the Kitchins, Larders, and Pasteries, know what meat's boil'd, bak'd, rost, stew'd, fri'd, or sous'd, at this dinner to be serv'd directly, or indirectly, to every several Table in the Court, be gone.

BOY

I run, but not so fast as your mouth will do upon the stroke of Eleven.

[Exit **BOY**.

LAZARELLO

What an excellent thing did God bestow upon man, when he did give him a good stomach! what unbounded graces there are pour'd upon them that have the continual command of the very best of these blessings! 'tis an excellent thing to be a Prince; he is serv'd with such admirable variety of Fare; such innumerable choice of Delicates; his Tables are full fraught with most nourishing food, and his Cubbards heavy laden with rich Wines; his Court is still filled with most pleasing varieties: In the Summer, his Palace is full of Green Geese; and in Winter it swarmeth Woodcocks,

Oh thou goddess of Plenty
Fill me this day with some rare delicates
And I will every year most constantly,
As this day celebrate a sumptuous Feast,
If thou wilt send me victuals in thine honor;
And to it shall be bidden for thy sake,
Even all the valiant stomachs in the Court:
All short-cloak'd Knights, and all cross-garter'd Gentlemen;
All pump and pantofle, foot-cloth riders;
With all the swarming generation
Of long stocks, short pain'd hose, and huge stuff'd doublets:
All these shall eat, and which is more than yet
Hath e'er been seen, they shall be satisfied.
I wonder my Ambassador returns not!

[Enter **BOY**.

BOY

Here I am Master.

LAZARELLO

And welcome:
Never did that sweet Virgin in her smock,
Fair-cheek'd Andromeda, when to the rock
Her Ivorie limbs were chain'd, and straight before
A huge Sea-monster, tumbling to the shore,
To have devour'd her, with more longing sight
Expect the coming of some hardy Knight,
That might have quell'd his pride, and set her free,

Than I with longing sight have look'd for thee.

BOY
Your Perseus is come Master, that will destroy him,
The very comfort of whose presence shuts
The monster hunger from your yelping guts.

LAZARELLO
Brief boy, brief, discourse the service of each several
Table compendiously.

BOY
Here's a Bill of all Sir.

LAZARELLO
Give it me, a Bill of all the several services this day appointed for every Table in the Court,
I, this is it on which my hopes relye,
Within this paper all my joyes are clos'd:
Boy, open it, and read it with reverence.

BOY
For the Captain of the Guards Table, three chines of Beef, and two jolls of Sturgeon.

LAZARELLO
A portly service, but gross, gross, proceed to the Dukes own Table, dear boy, to the Dukes own Table.

BOY
For the Dukes own Table, the head of an Umbrana.

LAZARELLO
Is't possible? can Heaven be so propitious to the Duke?

BOY
Yes, I'll assure you Sir, 'tis possible, Heaven is so propitious to him.

LAZARELLO
Why then he is the richest Prince alive:
He were the wealthiest Monarch in all Europe,
Had he no other Territories, Dominions, Provinces, Seats,
Nor Palaces, but only that Umbrana's head.

BOY
'Tis very fresh and sweet, Sir, the fish was taken but this night, and the head, as a rare novelty,
appointed by special commandement for the Dukes own Table, this dinner.

LAZARELLO
If poor unworthy I may come to eat
Of this most sacred dish, I here do vow

(If that blind Huswife, Fortune will bestow
But means on me) to keep a sumptuous house,

A board groaning under the heavy burden of the beasts that cheweth the cudd, and the Fowl that cutteth the Air: I shall not like the Table of a countrey Justice, besprinkled over with all manner of cheap Sallads, sliced Beef, Giblets, and Petitoes, to fill up room, nor should there stand any great, cumbersom, un-cut-up pies, at the nether end fill'd with moss and stones, partly to make a shew with and partly to keep the lower Mess from eating, nor shall my meat come in sneaking, like the City service, one dish a quarter of an hour after another, and gone, as if they had appointed to meet there, and had mistook the hour, nor should it, like the new Court service, come in haste, as if it fain would be gone again, all courses at once, like a hunting breakfast, but I would have my several courses, and my dishes well fill'd, my first course should be brought in after the antient manner, by a score of old bleer-ey'd Serving-men, in long blew coats, (marry they shall buy Silk, Facing, and Buttons themselves) but that's by the way.

BOY
Master the time calls on, will you be walking?

[Exit **BOY**.

LAZARELLO
Follow boy, follow, my guts were half an hour since in the privy Kitchin.

[Exeunt.

SCÆNA TERTIA

Enter **COUNT** and his Sister **ORIANA**.

ORIANA
Faith brother, I must needs go yonder.

COUNT
And faith Sister what will you do yonder?

ORIANA
I know the Lady Honoria will be glad to see me.

COUNT
Glad to see you? faith the Lady Honoria cares for you as she doth for all other young Ladies, she's glad to see you, and will shew you the Privy Garden, and tell you how many Gowns the Duchess had; Marry if you have ever an old Uncle, that would be a Lord, or ever a kinsman that hath done a murther, or committed a robbery, and will give good store of Money to procure his pardon, then the Lady Honoria will be glad to see you.

ORIANA
I, but they say one shall see fine sights at the Court.

COUNT

I'll tell you what you shall see, you shall see many faces of mans making, for you shall find very few as God left them: and you shall see many legs too; amongst the rest you shall behold one pair, the feet of which, were in times past, sockless, but are now through the change of time (that alters all things) very strangely become the legs of a Knight and a Courtier; another pair you shall see, that were heir apparent legs to a Glover, these legs hope shortly to be honourable; when they pass by they will bow, and the mouth to these legs, will seem to offer you some Courtship; it will swear, but it will lye, hear it not.

ORIANA

Why, and are not these fine sights?

COUNT

Sister, in seriousness you yet are young
And fair, a fair young Maid, and apt.

ORIANA

Apt?

COUNT

Exceeding apt, apt to be drawn to.

ORIANA

To what?

COUNT

To that you should not be, 'tis no dispraise,
She is not bad that hath desire to ill,
But she that hath no power to rule that Will:
For there you shall be wooed in other kinds
Than yet your years have known, the chiefest men
Will seem to throw themselves
As vassals at your service, kiss your hand,
Prepare you Banquets, Masques, Shews, all inticements
That Wit and Lust together can devise,
To draw a Lady from the state of Grace
To an old Lady widdows Gallery;
And they will praise your virtues, beware that,
The only way to turn a Woman whore,
Is to commend her chastity: you'll goe?

ORIANA

I would go, if it were but only to shew you, that I could be there, and be mov'd with none of these tricks.

COUNT

Your servants are ready?

ORIANA

An hour since.

COUNT
Well, if you come off clear from this hot service, Your praise shall be the greater. Farewel Sister.

ORIANA
Farewel Brother.

COUNT
Once more, if you stay in the presence till candle-light, keep on the foreside o'th' Curtain; and do you hear, take heed of the old Bawd, in the cloth of Tissue sleeves, and the knit Mittines. Farewel Sister.

[Exit **ORIANA**.

Now am I idle, I would I had been a Scholar, that I might a studied now: the punishment of meaner men is, they have too much to do; our only misery is, that without company we know not what to do; I must take some of the common courses of our Nobility; which is thus: if I can find no company that likes me, pluck off my Hatband, throw an old Cloak over my face, and as if I would not be known, walk hastily through the streets, till I be discovered; then there goes Count such a one, says one; there goes Count such a one, says another: Look how fast he goes, says a third; there's some great matters in hand questionless, says a fourth; when all my business is to have them say so: this hath been used; or if I can find any company, I'll after dinner to the Stage, to see a Play; where, when I first enter, you shall have a murmure in the house, every one that does not know cries, What Nobleman is that? all the Gallants on the Stage rise, vail to me, kiss their hand, offer me their places: then I pick out some one, whom I please to grace among the rest, take his seat, use it, throw my cloak over my face, and laugh at him: the poor Gentleman imagines himself most highly grac'd, thinks all the Auditors esteem him one of my bosom friends; and in right special regard with me. But here comes a Gentleman, that I hope will make me better sport, than either street and stage fooleries.

[Enter **LAZARELLO** and **BOY**.

This man loves to eat good meat, always provided, he do not pay for it himself, he goes by the name of the Hungry Courtier, marry, because I think that name will not sufficiently distinguish him, for no doubt he hath more fellows there, his name is Lazarello, he is none of these same ordinary eaters, that will devour three breakfasts, and as many dinners, without any prejudice to their Beavers, Drinkings, or Suppers; but he hath a more courtly kind of hunger, and doth hunt more after novelty, than plenty, I'll overhear him.

LAZARELLO
Oh thou most itching kindly appetite,
Which every creature in his stomach feels;
Oh leave, leave yet at last thus to torment me.
Three several Sallads have I sacrific'd,
Bedew'd with precious oil and vinegar
Already to appease thy greedy wrath. Boy.

BOY
Sir.

LAZARELLO
Will the Count speak with me?

BOY
One of his Gentlemen is gone to inform him of your coming, Sir.

LAZARELLO
There is no way left for me to compass this Fish-head, but by being presently made known to the Duke.

BOY
That will be hard Sir.

LAZARELLO
When I have tasted of this sacred dish,
Then shall my bones rest in my Fathers tomb
In peace; then shall I dye most willingly,
And as a dish be serv'd to satisfie,
Deaths hunger, and I will be buried thus:
My Bier shall be a charger born by four,
The Coffin where I lye, a powd'ring-tub,
Bestrew'd with Lettice, and cool Sallad herbs,
My Winding-sheet of Tansies, the black Guard
Shall be my solemn Mourners, and instead
Of ceremonies, wholsom burial Prayers:
A printed dirge in rhyme, shall bury me.
Instead of tears, let them pour Capon sauce upon my hearse,
And salt instead of dust, Manchets for stones, for other glorious shields
Give me a Voider; and above my Hearse
For a Trutch sword, my naked knife stuck up.

[The **COUNT** discovers himself.

BOY
Master, the Count's here.

LAZARELLO
Where? my Lord I do beseech you.

COUNT
Y'are very welcome Sir, I pray you stand up, you shall dine with me.

LAZARELLO
I do beseech your Lordship by the love I still have born to your honourable house.

COUNT
Sir, what need all this? you shall dine with me, I pray rise.

LAZARELLO

Perhaps your Lordship takes me for one of these same fellows, that do as it were respect victuals.

COUNT

Oh Sir by no means.

LAZARELLO

Your Lordship has often promised, that whensoever I should affect greatness, your own hand should help to raise me.

COUNT

And so much still assure your self of.

LAZARELLO

And though I must confess, I have ever shun'd popularity, by the example of others, yet I do now feel my self a little ambitious, your Lordship is great, and though young, yet a Privy Counsellor.

COUNT

I pray you Sir leap into the matter, what would You have me do for you?

LAZARELLO

I would intreat your Lordship to make me known to the Duke.

COUNT

When Sir?

LAZARELLO

Suddainly my Lord, I would have you present me unto him this morning.

COUNT

It shall be done, but for what virtues, would you have him take notice of you?

LAZARELLO

Your Lordship shall know that presently.

COUNT

'Tis pity of this fellow, he is of good wit, and sufficient understanding, when he is not troubled with this greedy worm.

LAZARELLO

'Faith, you may intreat him to take notice of me for any thing; for being an excellent Farrier, for playing well at Span-counter, or sticking knives in walls, for being impudent, or for nothing; why may not I be a Favorite on the suddain? I see nothing against it.

COUNT

Not so Sir, I know you have not the face to be a Favourite on the suddain.

LAZARELLO

Why then you shall present me as a Gentleman well qualified, or one extraordinary seen in divers strange mysteries.

COUNT
In what Sir? as how?

LAZARELLO
Marry as thus—

[Enter **INTELLIGENCER**.

COUNT
Yonder's my old Spirit, that hath haunted me daily, ever since I was a privy Counsellor, I must be rid of him, I pray you stay there, I am a little busie, I will speak with you presently.

LAZARELLO
You shall bring me in, and after a little other talk taking me by the hand, you shall utter these words to the Duke: May it please your grace, to take note of a Gentleman, well read, deeply learned, and throughly grounded in the hidden knowledge of all Sallads and Pot-herbs whatsoever.

COUNT
'Twill be rare, if you will walk before, Sir, I will overtake you instantly.

LAZARELLO
Your Lordships ever.

COUNT
This fellow is a kind of an informer, one that lives in Alehouses and Taverns, and because he perceives some worthy men in this Land, with much labour and great expence, to have discovered things dangerously hanging over the State; he thinks to discover as much out of the talk of drunkards in Tap-houses: he brings me informations, pick'd out of broken words, in mens common talk, which, with his malicious mis-application, he hopes will seem dangerous, he doth besides, bring me the names of all the young Gentlemen in the City, that use Ordinaries, or Taverns, talking (to my thinking) only as the freedom of their youth teach them, without any further ends; for dangerous and seditious spirits; he is besides, an arrant whoremaster, as any is in Milan, of a Lay-man; I will not meddle with the Clergy: he is parcel Lawyer, and in my conscience much of their religion, I must put upon him some piece of service; come hither Sir, what have you to do with me?

INTELLIGENCER
Little my Lord, I only come to know how your Lordship would employ me.

COUNT
Observed you that Gentleman, that parted from me but now?

INTELLIGENCER
I saw him now my Lord.

COUNT

I was sending for you, I have talked with this man, and I do find him dangerous.

INTELLIGENCER
Is your Lordship in good earnest?

COUNT
Hark you Sir, there may perhaps be some within ear-shot.
He whispers with him.

[Enter **LAZARELLO** and his **BOY**.

LAZARELLO
Sirrah, will you venture your life, the Duke hath sent the
Fish-head to my Lord?

BOY
Sir if he have not, kill me, do what you will with me.

LAZARELLO
How uncertain is the state of all mortal things! I have these crosses from my Cradle, from my very
Cradle, insomuch that I do begin to grow desperate: Fortune I do despise thee, do thy worst; yet when I
do better gather my self together, I do find it is rather the part of a wise man, to prevent the storms of
Fortune by stirring, than to suffer them by standing still, to pour themselves upon his naked body. I will
about it.

COUNT
Who's within there?

[Enter a **SERVINGMAN**.

Let this Gentleman out at the back door, forget not my instructions, if you find any thing dangerous;
trouble not your self to find out me, but carry your informations to the Lord Lucio, he is a man grave,
and well experienced in these businesses.

INTELLIGENCER
Your Lordships Servant.

[Exit **INTELLIGENCER** and **SERVINGMAN**.

LAZARELLO
Will it please your worship walke?

COUNT
Sir I was coming, I will overtake you.

LAZARELLO
I will attend you over against the Lord Gonderinoes house.

COUNT
You shall not attend there long.

LAZARELLO
Thither must I to see my Loves face, the chaste
Virgin head
Of a dear Fish, yet pure and undeflowred,
Not known of man no rough bred countrey hand,
Hath once toucht thee, no Pandars withered paw,
Nor an un-napkin'd Lawyers greasie fist,
Hath once slubbered thee: no Ladies supple hand,
Wash'd o'er with Urine, hath yet seiz'd on thee
With her two nimble talents: no Court hand,
Whom his own natural filth, or change of air,
Hath bedeck'd with scabs, hath marr'd thy whiter grace:
Oh let it be thought lawful then for me,
To crop the flower of thy Virginity.

[Exit **LAZARELLO**.

COUNT
This day I am for fools, I am all theirs,
Though like to our young wanton cocker'd heirs,
Who do affect those men above the rest,
In whose base company they still are best:
I do not with much labour strive to be
The wisest ever in the company:
But for a fool, our wisdom oft amends,
As enemies do teach us more than friends.

[Exit **COUNT**.

ACTUS SECUNDUS

SCENA PRIMA

Enter **GONDARINO** and his **SERVANTS**.

SERVANT
My Lord:

GONDARINO
Ha!

SERVANT
Here's one hath brought you a present.

GONDARINO

From whom? from a woman? if it be from a woman, bid him carrie it back, and tell her she's a whore; what is it?

SERVANT

A Fish head my Lord.

GONDARINO

What Fish head?

SERVANT

I did not aske that my Lord.

GONDARINO

Whence comes it?

SERVANT

From the Court.

GONDARINO

O 'tis a Cods-head.

SERVANT

No my Lord, 'tis some strange head, it comes from the Duke.

GONDARINO

Let it be carried to my Mercer, I doe owe him money for silks, stop his mouth with that.

[Exit **SERVANT**.

Was there ever any man that hated his wife after death but I? and for her sake all women, women that were created only for the preservation of little dogs.

[Enter **SERVANT**.

SERVANT

My Lord the Count's sister being overtaken in the streets, with a great hail-storm, is light at your gate, and desires room till the storm be overpast.

GONDARINO

Is she a woman?

SERVANT

I my Lord I think so.

GONDARINO

I have none for her then: bid her get her gone, tell her she is not welcome.

SERVANT

My Lord, she is now comming up.

GONDARINO

She shall not come up, tell her any thing; tell her I have but one great room in my house, and I am now in it at the close stool.

SERVANT

She's here my Lord.

GONDARINO

O impudence of women: I can keep dogs out of my house, or I can defend my house against theeves, but I cannot keep out women.

[Enter **ORIANA**, a waiting woman, and a **PAGE**.

Now Madam, what hath your Ladyship to say to me?

ORIANA

My Lord, I was bold to crave the help of your house against the storm.

GONDARINO

Your Ladyships boldness in coming will be impudence in staying; for you are most unwelcome.

ORIANA

Oh my Lord!

GONDARINO

Doe you laugh? by the hate I bear to you, 'tis true.

ORIANA

Y'are merry my Lord.

GONDARINO

Let me laugh to death if I be, or can be whilst thou art here, or livest; or any of thy sex.

ORIANA

I commend your Lordship.

GONDARINO

Doe you commend me? why doe you commend me? I give you no such cause: thou art a filthy impudent whore; a woman, a very woman.

ORIANA

Ha, ha, ha.

GONDARINO

Begot when thy father was drunk.

ORIANA
Your Lordship hath a good wit.

GONDARINO
How? what have I a good wit?

ORIANA
Come my Lord, I have heard before of your Lordships merry vain in jesting against our Sex, which I being desirous to hear, made me rather choose your Lordships house, than any other, but I know I am welcome.

GONDARINO
Let me not live if you be: me thinks it doth not become you, to come to my house being a stranger to you, I have no woman in my house, to entertain you, nor to shew you your chamber; why should you come to me? I have no Galleries, nor banqueting houses, nor bawdy pictures to shew your Ladyship.

ORIANA
Believe me this your Lordships plainness makes me think my self more welcome, than if you had sworn by all the pretty Court oaths that are, I had been welcomer than your soul to your body.

GONDARINO
Now she's in, talking treason will get her out, I durst sooner undertake to talk an Intelligencer out of the room, and speak more than he durst hear, than talk a woman out of my company.

[Enter a **SERVANT**.

SERVANT
My Lord the Duke being in the streets, and the storm continuing, is entred your gate, and now coming up.

GONDARINO
The Duke! now I know your Errand Madam; you have plots and private meetings in hand: why doe you choose my house? are you asham'd to goe to't in the old coupling place, though it be less suspicious here; for no Christian will suspect a woman to be in my house? yet you may do it cleanlyer there, for there is a care had of those businesses; and wheresoever you remove, your great maintainer and you shall have your lodgings directly opposite, it is but putting on your night-gown, and your slippers; Madam, you understand me?

ORIANA
Before I would not understand him, but now he speaks riddles to me indeed.

[Enter the **DUKE**, **ARRIGO** and **LUCIO**.

DUKE
'Twas a strange hail-storm.

LUCIO
'Twas exceeding strange.

GONDARINO
Good morrow to your grace.

DUKE
Good morrow Gonderino.

GONDARINO
Justice great Prince.

DUKE
Why should you beg for justice, I never did you wrong;
What's the offendor?

GONDARINO
A woman.

DUKE
I know your ancient quarrell against that Sex; but what hainous crime hath she committed?

GONDARINO
She hath gone abroad.

DUKE
What? it cannot be.

GONDARINO
She hath done it.

DUKE
How? I never heard of any woman that did so before.

GONDARINO
If she have not laid by that modesty
That should attend a Virgin, and, quite void
Of shame, hath left the house where she was born,
As they should never doe; let me endure
The pains that she should suffer.

DUKE
Hath she so? Which is the woman?

GONDARINO
This, this.

DUKE

How! Arrigo? Lucio?

GONDARINO
I then it is a plot, no Prince alive
Shall force me make my house a Brothell house;
Not for the sins, but for the womans sake,
I will not have her in my doors so long:
Will they make my house as bawdy as their own are?

DUKE
Is it not Oriana?

LUCIO
'Tis.

DUKE
Sister to Count Valero?

ARRIGO
The very same.

DUKE
She that I love?

LUCIO
She that you love.

DUKE
I do suspect.

LUCIO
So doe I.

DUKE
This fellow to be but a counterfeit,
One that doth seem to loath all woman-kind,
To hate himself, because he hath some part
Of woman in him; seems not to endure
To see, or to be seen of any woman,
Only, because he knows it is their nature
To wish to tast that which is most forbidden:
And with this shew he may the better compass
(And with far less suspition) his base ends.

LUCIO
Upon my life 'tis so.

DUKE

And I doe know,
Before his slain wife gave him that offence,
He was the greatest servant to that Sex
That ever was: what doth this Lady here
With him alone? why should he rail at her to me?

LUCIO
Because your grace might not suspect.

DUKE
'Twas so: I doe love her strangely:
I would fain know the truth: counsell me.

[They three whisper.

[Enter **COUNT**, **LAZARELLO** and his **BOY**.

COUNT
It falls out better than we could expect Sir, that we should find the Duke and my Lord Gondarino together; both which you desire to be acquainted with.

LAZARELLO
'Twas very happy: Boy, goe down into the kitchen, and see if you can spy that same; I am now in some hope: I have me thinks a kind of fever upon me.

[Exit **BOY**.

A certain gloominess within me, doubting as it were, betwixt two passions: there is no young maid upon her wedding night, when her husband sets first foot in the bed, blushes, and looks pale again, oftner than I doe now. There is no Poet acquainted with more shakings and quakings, towards the latter end of his new play, when he's in that case, that he stands peeping betwixt the Curtains, so fearfully that a Bottle of Ale cannot be opened, but he thinks some body hisses, than I am at this instant.

COUNT
Are they in consultation? If they be, either my young Duke hath gotten some Bastard, and is persuading my Knight yonder to father the child, and marry the wench, or else some Cock-pit is to be built.

LAZARELLO
My Lord! what Nobleman's that?

COUNT
His name is Lucio, 'tis he that was made a Lord at the request of some of his friends for his wives sake: he affects to be a great States-man, and thinks it consists in night-caps and jewells, and tooth-picks.

LAZARELLO
And what's that other?

COUNT

A Knight Sir, that pleaseth the Duke to favour, and to raise to some extraordinary fortunes, he can make as good men as himself, every day in the week, and doth—

LAZARELLO
For what was he raised?

COUNT
Truely Sir, I am not able to say directly, for what; But for wearing of red breeches as I take it; he's a brave man, he will spend three Knighthoods at a Supper without Trumpets.

LAZARELLO
My Lord I'll talk with him, for I have a friend, that would gladly receive the humor.

COUNT
If he have the itch of Knighthood upon him, let him repair to that Physitian, he'll cure him: but I will give you a note; is your friend fat or lean?

LAZARELLO
Something fat.

COUNT
'Twill be the worse for him.

LAZARELLO
I hope that's not material.

COUNT
Very much, for there is an impost set upon Knighthoods, & your friend shall pay a Noble in the pound.

DUKE
I doe not like examinations,
We shall find out the truth more easily,
Some other way less noted, and that course,
Should not be us'd, till we be sure to prove
Some thing directly, for when they perceive
Themselves suspected, they will then provide
More warily to answer.

LUCIO
Doth she know your Grace doth love her?

DUKE
She hath never heard it.

LUCIO
Then thus my Lord.

[They whisper

LAZARELLO

What's he that walks alone so sadly with his hands behind him?

COUNT

The Lord of the house, he that you desire to be acquainted with, he doth hate women for the same cause that I love them.

LAZARELLO

What's that?

COUNT

For that which Apes want: you perceive me Sir?

LAZARELLO

And is he sad? Can he be sad that hath so rich a gem under his roof, as that which I doe follow. What young Lady's that?

COUNT

Which? Have I mine eye-sight perfect, 'tis my sister: did I say the Duke had a Bastard? What should she make here with him and his Councell? She hath no papers in her hand to petition to them, she hath never a husband in prison, whose release she might sue for: That's a fine trick for a wench; to get her husband clapt up, that she may more freely, and with less suspition, visit the private studies of men in authority. Now I doe discover their consultation, yon fellow is a Pander without all salvation: But let me not condemn her too rashly without weighing the matter; she's a young Lady, she went forth early this morning with a waiting woman, and a Page, or so: This is no garden house; in my conscience she went forth with no dishonest intent: for she did not pretend going to any Sermon in the further end of the City: Neither went she to see any odd old Gentlewoman, that mourns for the death of her husband, or the loss of her friend, and must have young Ladys come to comfort her: those are the damnable Bawds: 'Twas no set meeting certainly; for there was no wafer-woman with her these three days on my knowledge: I'll talk with her; Good morrow my Lord.

GONDARINO

Y'are welcome Sir: here's her brother come now to doe a kind office for his sister; is it not strange?

COUNT

I am glad to meet you here sister.

ORIANA

I thank you good brother: and if you doubt of the cause of my coming I can satisfie you.

COUNT

No faith, I dare trust thee, I doe suspect thou art honest; for it is so rare a thing to be honest amongst you, that some one man in an age, may perhaps suspect some two women to be honest, but never believe it verily.

LUCIO

Let your return be suddain.

ARRIGO
Unsuspected by them.

DUKE
It shall; so shall I best perceive their Love, if there be any; Farewell.

COUNT
Let me entreat your grace to stay a little,
To know a gentleman, to whom your self
Is much beholding; he hath made the sport
For your whole Court these eight years, on my knowledge.

DUKE
His name?

COUNT
Lazarello.

DUKE
I heard of him this morning, which is he?

COUNT
Lazarello, pluck up thy spirits, thy Fortuns are now raising, the Duke calls for thee, and thou shalt be acquainted with him.

LAZARELLO
He's going away, and I must of necessity stay here upon business.

COUNT
'Tis all one, thou shalt know him first.

LAZARELLO
Stay a little, if he should offer to take me away with him, and by that means I should loose that I seek for; but if he should I will not goe with him.

COUNT
Lazarello, the Duke stayes, wilt thou lose this opportunity?

LAZARELLO
How must I speak to him?

COUNT
'Twas well thought of: you must not talk to him as you doe to an ordinary man, honest plain sence, but you must wind about him: for example, if he should aske you what a clock it is, you must not say; If it please your grace 'tis nine; but thus; thrice three a clock, so please my Sovereign: or thus;

Look how many Muses there doth dwell

Upon the sweet banks of the learned Well;
And just so many stroaks the clock hath struck,
And so forth; And you must now and then enter into a description.

LAZARELLO
I hope I shall doe it.

COUNT
Come: May it please your grace to take note of a Gentleman, wel seen, deeply read, and throughly grounded in the hidden knowledge of all sallets and potherbs whatsoever.

DUKE
I shall desire to know him more inwardly.

LAZARELLO
I kiss the Oxe-hide of your graces foot.

COUNT
Very well: will your grace question him a little?

DUKE
How old are you?

LAZARELLO
Full eight and twenty several Almanacks
Have been compiled, all for several years
Since first I drew this breath, four prentiships
Have I most truely served in this world:
And eight and twenty times hath Phœbus Car
Run out his yearly course since.

DUKE
I understand you Sir.

LUCIO
How like an ignorant Poet he talks.

DUKE
You are eight and twenty yeare old? what time of the day doe you hold it to be?

LAZARELLO
About the time that mortals whet their knives
On thresholds, on their shooe soles, and on stairs,
New bread is grating, and the testy Cook
Hath much to doe now, now the Tables all.

DUKE
'Tis almost dinner time?

LAZARELLO

Your grace doth apprehend me very rightly.

COUNT

Your grace shall find him in your further conference
Grave, wise, courtly, and scholar like, understandingly read
In the necessities of the life of man.
He knows that man is mortal by his birth;
He knows that man must dye, and therefore live;
He knows that man must live, and therefore eat,
And if it shall please your grace, to accompany your self with him, I doubt not, but that he will, at the least, make good my commendations.

DUKE

Attend us Lazarello, we doe want
Men of such Action, as we have received you
Reported from your honorable friend.

LAZARELLO

Good my Lord stand betwixt me and my overthrow, you know I'm ti'd here, and may not depart, my gracious Lord, so waightie are the businesses of mine own, which at this time do call upon me, that I will rather chuse to die, than to neglect them.

COUNT

Nay you shall well perceive, besides the virtues that I have alreadie inform'd you of, he hath a stomach which will stoop to no Prince alive.

DUKE

Sir at your best leisure, I shall thirst to see you.

LAZARELLO

And I shall hunger for it.

DUKE

Till then farewell all.

GONGARINO

Count
Long life attend your Grace.

DUKE

I doe not tast this sport, Arrigo, Lucio.

ARRIGO, LUCIO

We doe attend.

[Exeunt **DUKE**, **ARRIGO**, **LUCIO**.

GONDARINO

His grace is gone, and hath left his Hellen with me, I'm no pander for him, neither can I be won with the hope of gain, or the itching desire of tasting my Lords lecherie to him, to keep her at (my house) or bring her in disguise, to his bed Chamber.

The twyns of Adders, and of Scorpions
About my naked brest, will seem to me
More tickling than those claspes, which men adore;
The lustfull, dull, ill spirited embraces
Of women; The much praysed Amazones,
Knowing their own infirmities so well,
Made of themselves a people, and what men
They take amongst them, they condemne to die,
Perceiving that their folly made them fit
To live no longer that would willingly
Come in the worthless presence of a woman.
I will attend, and see what my young Lord will doe with his sister.

[Enter Lazarello's **BOY**.

BOY

My Lord; The fish head is gone again.

COUNT

Whither?

BOY

I know whither my Lord.

COUNT

Keep it from Lazarillo: Sister shall I confer with you in private, to know the cause of the Dukes coming hither, I know he makes you acquainted with his business of State.

ORIANA

I'll satisfie you brother, for I see you are jealous of me.

GONDARINO

Now there shall be some course taken for her conveiance.

LAZARELLO

Lazarillo, thou art happy, thy carriage hath begot love, and that love hath brought forth fruits; thou art here in the company of a man honorable, that will help thee to tast of the bounties of the Sea, and when thou hast so done thou shalt retire thy self unto the court, and there tast of the delicates of the earth, and be great in the eyes of thy Soveraign: now no more shalt thou need to scramble for thy meat, nor remove thy stomach with the Court; But thy credit shall command thy hearts desire, and all novelties shall be sent as presents unto thee.

COUNT

Good Sister, when you see your own time, will you return home.

ORIANA
Yes brother, and not before.

LAZARELLO
I will grow popular in this State, and overthrow the fortunes of a number, that live by extortion.

COUNT
Lazarello, bestirr thy self nimbly and sodainly, and hear me with patience to hear.

LAZARELLO
Let me not fall from my self; Speak I'm bound.

COUNT
So art thou to revenge, when thou shalt hear the fish head is gone, and we know not whither.

LAZARELLO
I will not curse, nor swear, nor rage, nor rail,
Nor with contemptuous tongue, accuse my Fate;
Though I might justly doe it, nor will I
Wish my self uncreated for this evil:
Shall I entreat your Lordship to be seen
A little longer in the company
Of a man cross'd by Fortune?

COUNT
I hate to leave my friend in his extremities.

LAZARELLO
'Tis noble in you, then I take your hand,
And doe protest, I doe not follow this
For any malice or for private ends,
But with a love, as gentle and as chast,
As that a brother to his sister bears:
And if I see this fish head yet unknown;
The last words that my dying father spake,
Before his eye strings brake, shall not of me
So often be remembred, as our meeting:
Fortune attend me, as my ends are just,
Full of pure love, and free from servile lust.

COUNT
Farwell my Lord, I was entreated to invite your Lordship to a Lady's upsiting.

GONDARINO
O my ears, why Madam, will not you follow your brother? You are waited for by great men, heel bring you to him.

ORIANA

I'm very well my Lord, you doe mistake me, if you think I affect greater company than your self.

GONDARINO

What madness possesseth thee, that thou canst imagine me a fit man to entertain Ladies; I tell thee, I doe use to tear their hair, to kick them, and to twindge their noses, if they be not carefull in avoiding me.

ORIANA

Your Lordship may discant upon your own behavior as please you, but I protest, so sweet and courtly it appeares in my eye, that I mean not to leave you yet.

GONDARINO

I shall grow rough.

ORIANA

A rough carriage is best in a man,
I'll dine with you my Lord.

GONDARINO

Why I will starve thee, thou shalt have nothing.

ORIANA

I have heard of your Lordships nothing, I'll put that to the venture.

GONDARINO

Well thou shalt have meat, I'll send it to thee.

ORIANA

I'll keep no state my Lord, neither doe I mourn, I'll dine with you.

GONDARINO

Is such a thing as this allowed to live?
What power hath let thee loose upon the earth
To plague us for our Sins? Out of my doors.

ORIANA

I would your Lordship did but see how well
This fury doth become you, it doth shew
So neer the life, as it were natural.

GONDARINO

O thou damn'd woman, I will flie the vengeance
That hangs above thee, follow if thou dar'st.

[Exit **GONDARINO**.

ORIANA
I must not leave this fellow, I will torment him to madness,
To teach his passions against kind to move,
The more he hates, the more I'll seem to love.

[Exeunt **ORIANA** and **MAID**.

[Enter **PANDAR** and **MERCER** a citizen.

PANDAR
Sir, what may be done by art shall be done, I wear not this black cloak for nothing.

MERCER
Perform this, help me to this great heir by learning, and you shall want no black cloaks; taffaties, silkgrograms, sattins and velvets are mine, they shall be yours; perform what you have promis'd, and you shall make me a lover of Sciences, I will study the learned languages, and keep my shop-book in Latine.

PANDAR
Trouble me not now, I will not fail you within this hour at your shop.

MERCER
Let Art have her course.

[Exit **MERCER**.

[Enter **CURTEZAN**.

PANDAR
'Tis well spoken, Madona.

MADONA
Hast thou brought me any customers.

PANDAR
No.

MADONA
What the devil do'st thou in black?

PANDAR
As all solemn professors of setled courses, doe cover my knavery with it: will you marry a citizen; Reasonably rich, and unreasonably foolish, silks in his shop, mony in his purse, and no wit in his head?

MADONA
Out upon him, I could have bin otherwise than so, there was a Knight swore he would have had me, if I would have lent him but forty shillings to have redeem'd his cloak, to goe to Church in.

PANDAR
Then your wastcote wayter shall have him, call her in!

MADONA
Francessina!

FRANCESSINA
Anon!

MADONNA
Get you to the Church, and shrive your self,
For you shall be richly marryed anon.

PANDAR
And get you after her, I will work upon my citizen whilst he is warm, I must not suffer him to consult with his neighbours, the openest fools are hardly cousened, if they once grow jealous.

[Exeunt.

ACTUS TERTIUS

SCÆNA PRIMA

Enter **GONDARINO** flying the Lady.

GONDARINO
Save me ye better powers, let me not fall
Between the loose embracements of a woman:
Heaven, if my Sins be ripe grown to a head,
And must attend your vengeance: I beg not to divert my fate,
Or to reprive a while thy punishment
Only I crave, and hear me equall heavens,
Let not your furious rod, that must afflict me
Be that imperfect peece of nature,
That art makes up, woman, unsatiate woman.
Had we not knowing souls, at first infus'd
To teach a difference, 'twixt extremes and goods?
Were we not made our selves, free, unconfin'd
Commanders of our own affections?
And can it be, that this most perfect creature,
This image of his maker, well squar'd man,
Should leave the handfast, that he had of grace,
To fall into a womans easie armes.

[Enter **ORIANA**.

ORIANA

Now Venus, be my speed, inspire me with all the severall subtil temptations, that thou hast already given, or hast in store heareafter to bestow upon our Sex: grant that I may apply that Physick that is most apt to work upon him: whether he will soonest be mov'd with wantonness, singing, dancing; or being passionate, with scorn; or with sad and serious looks, cunningly mingled with sighs, with smiling, lisping, kissing the hand, and making short curt'sies, Or with whatsoever other nimble power, he may be caught, doe thou infuse into me, and when I have him, I will sacrifice him up to thee.

GONDARINO

It comes again; New apparitions,
And tempting spirits: Stand and reveal thy self,
Tell why thou followest me! I fear thee
As I fear the place thou cam'st from: Hell.

ORIANA

My Lord, I 'm a woman, and such a one—

GONDARINO

That I hate truely, thou hadst better bin a devill.

ORIANA

Why my unpatient Lord?

GONDARINO

Devils were once good, there they excell'd you women.

ORIANA

Can ye be so uneasie, can ye freeze, and
Such a summers heat so ready
To dissolve? nay gentle Lord, turn not away in scorn,
Nor hold me less fair than I am: look on these cheeks,
They have yet enough of nature, true complexion,
If to be red and white, a forehead high,
An easie melting lip, a speaking eye,
And such a tongue, whose language takes the ear
Of strict religion, and men most austere:
If these may hope to please, look here.

GONDARINO

This woman with entreaty wo'd show all,
Lady there lies your way, I pray ye farewell.

ORIANA

Y'are yet too harsh, too dissonant,
There's no true musick in your words, my Lord.

GONDARINO

What shall I give thee to be gone?

Here's ta, and tha wants lodging, take my house, 'tis big enough, 'tis thine own, 'twill hold five leacherous Lords, and their lackies without discovery: there's stoves and bathing tubs.

ORIANA

Dear Lord: y'are too wild.

GONDARINO

Shalt have a Doctor too, thou shalt, 'bout six and twentie, 'tis a pleasing age; Or I can help thee to a handsome Usher: or if thou lack'st a page, I'll give thee one, preethee keep house, and leave me.

ORIANA

I doe confess I'm too easie, too much woman,
Not coy enough to take affection,
Yet I can frown and nip a passion,
Even in the bud: I can say
Men please their present heats; Then please to leave us.
I can hold off, and, by my Chymick power,
Draw Sonnets from the melting lovers brain;
Ayme's, and Elegies: yet to you my Lord
My Love, my better self, I put these off,
Doing that office, not befits our sex,
Entreat a man to love;
Are ye not yet relenting? ha'ye blood and Spirit
In those veins? ye are no image, though ye be as hard
As marble: sure ye have no liver, if ye had,
'Twould send a lively and desiring heat
To every member; Is not this miserable?
A thing so truely form'd, shapt out by Symetry,
Has all the organs that belong to man,
And working too, yet to shew all these
Like dead motions moving upon wyers?
Then good my Lord, leave off what you have been,
And freely be what you were first intended for, a man.

GONDARINO

Thou art a precious peece of slie damnation,
I will be deaf, I will lock up my ears,
Tempt me not, I will not love; If I doe.

ORIANA

Then I'll hate you.

GONDARINO

Let me be 'nointed with hony, and turn'd into the Sun,
To be stung to death with horse-flies,
Hear'st thou, thou breeder, here I'll sit,
And, in despight of thee, I will say nothing.

ORIANA

Let me with your fair patience, sit beside you.

GONDARINO

Madam, Lady, tempter, tongue, woman, ayr.
Look to me, I shall kick; I say again,
Look to me I shall kick.

ORIANA

I cannot think your better knowledge can use a woman so uncivilly.

GONDARINO

I cannot think, I shall become a coxcombe,
To ha'my hair curl'd, by an idle finger,
My cheeks turn Tabers, and be plaid upon,
Mine eyes lookt babies in, and my nose blowd to my hand,
I say again I shall kick, sure I shall.

ORIANA

'Tis but your outside that you shew, I know your mind
Never was guilty of so great a weakness,
Or could the tongues of all men joyn'd together.
Possess me with a thought of your dislike
My weakness were above a womans, to fall off
From my affection, for one crack of thunder,
O wo'd you could love, my Lord.

GONDARINO

I wo'd thou wouldst sit still, and say nothing: what mad-man let thee loose to do more mischief than a dousen whirlwinds, keep thy hands in thy muff, and warm the idle worms in thy fingers ends: will ye be doing still? will no entreating serve ye? no lawfull warning? I must remove and leave your Ladyship; Nay never hope to stay me, for I will run, from that Smooth, Smiling, Witching, Cousening, Tempting, Damning face of thine, as far as I can find any land, where I will put my self into a daily course of Curses for thee, and all thy Familie.

ORIANA

Nay good my Lord sit still, I'll promise peace
And fold mine Armes up, let but mine eye discourse;
Or let my voyce, set to some pleasing cord, sound out
The sullen strains of my neglected love.

GONDARINO

Sing till thou crack thy treble-string in peeces,
And when thou hast done, put up thy pipes and walk,
Doe any thing, sit still and tempt me not.

ORIANA

I had rather sing at doors for bread, than sing to this fellow, but for hate: if this should be told in the Court, that I begin to woe Lords, what a troop of the untrust nobilitie should I have at my lodging to morrow morning.

SONG.
Come sleep, and with thy sweet deceiving,
Lock me in delight a while,
Let some pleasing Dreams beguile
All my fancies; That from thence,
I may feel an influence,
All my powers of care bereaving.
Though but a shadow, but a sliding,
Let me know some little Joy,
We that suffer long anoy
Are contented with a thought
Through an idle fancie wrought
O let my joyes, have some abiding.

GONDARINO
Have you done your wassayl? 'tis a handsome drowsie dittie I'll assure ye, now I had as leave hear a Cat cry, when her tail is cut off, as hear these lamentations, these lowsie love-layes, these bewailements: you think you have caught me Lady, you think I melt now, like a dish of May butter, and run, all into brine, and passion, yes, yes, I 'm taken, look how I cross my arms, look pale, and dwyndle, and wo'd cry, but for spoyling my face; we must part, nay we'll avoyd all Ceremony, no kissing Lady, I desire to know your Ladiship no more; death of my soul the Duke!

ORIANA
God keep your Lordship.

GONDARINO
From thee and all thy sex.

ORIANA
I'll be the Clark, and crie, Amen,
Your Lordships ever assured enemie Oriana.

[Exit. **ORIANA**, Manet **GONDARINO**.

SCÆNA SECONDA

Enter **DUKE**, **ARRIGO**, **LUCIO**.

GONDARINO
All the days good, attend your Lordship.

DUKE

We thank you Gondarino, is it possible?
Can belief lay hold on such a miracle,
To see thee, one that hath cloyst'red up all passion,
Turn'd wilfull votary, and forsworn converse with women, in company and fair discourse, with the best beauty of Millain?

GONDARINO
'Tis true, and if your Grace that hath the sway
Of the whole State, will suffer this lude sex,
These women, to pursue us to our homes,
Not to be prayd, nor to be rail'd away,
But they will woe, and dance, and sing,
And, in a manner, looser than they are
By nature (which should seem impossible)
To throw their armes, on our unwilling necks.

DUKE
No more, I can see through your vissore, dissemble it no more.
Doe not I know thou hast us'd all Art,
To work upon the poor simplicitie
Of this yong Maid, that yet hath known none ill?
Thinkest that damnation will fright those that wooe
From oaths, and lies? But yet I think her chast,
And will from thee, before thou shalt apply
Stronger temptations, bear her hence with me.

GONDARINO
My Lord, I speak not this to gain new grace,
But howsoever you esteeme my words,
My love and dutie will not suffer me
To see you favour such a prostitute,
And I stand by dumb; Without Rack, Torture,
Or Strappado, Ile unrip my self:
I doe confess I was in company with that pleasing peece of frailtie, that we call woman; I doe confess after a long and tedious seige, I yielded.

DUKE
Forward.

GONDARINO
Faith my Lord to come quickly to the point, the woman you saw with me is a whore; An arrant whore.

DUKE
Was she not Count Valores Sister?

GONDARINO
Yes, that Count Valores Sister is naught.

DUKE
Thou dar'st not say so.

GONDARINO
Not if it be distasting to your Lordship, but give me freedome, and I dare maintain, she ha's imbrac'd this body, and grown to it as close, as the hot youthfull vine to the elme.

DUKE
Twice have I seen her with thee, twice my thoughts were prompted by mine eye, to hold thy strictness false and imposterous: Is this your mewing up, your strict retirement, your bitterness and gaul against that sex? Have I not heard thee say, thou wouldst sooner meet the Basilisks dead doing eye, than meet a woman for an object? Look it be true you tell me, or by our countries Saint your head goes off: if thou prove a whore, no womans face shall ever move me more.

[Exeunt. Manet **GONDARINO**.

GONDARINO
So, so, 'tis as 't should be, are women grown so mankind? Must they be wooing, I have a plot shall blow her up, she flyes, she mounts; I'll teach her Ladyship to dare my fury, I will be known, and fear'd, and more truely hated of women than an Eunuch.

[Enter **ORIANA**.

She's here again, good gaul be patient, for I must dissemble.

ORIANA
Now my cold, frosty Lord, my woman-Hater, you that have sworn an everlasting hate to all our sex: by my troth good Lord, and as I'm yet a maid, my thought 'twas excellent sport to hear your honor swear out an Alphabet, chafe nobly like a Generall, kick like a resty Jade, and make ill faces: Did your good Honor think I was in love? where did I first begin to take that heat? From those two radiant eyes, that piercing sight? oh they were lovely, if the balls stood right; and there's a leg made out of a dainty staff. Where, the Gods be thanked, there is calf enough.

GONDARINO
Pardon him Lady, that is now a convertite.
Your beauty, like a Saint hath wrought this wonder.

ORIANA
Alass, ha's it been prick'd at the heart? is the stomach come down? will it rail no more at women, and call 'em Divells, she Cats, and Goblins?

GONDARINO
He that shall marry thee, had better spend the poor remainder of his days in a dung-barge, for two pence a week, and find him self.

Down again Spleen, I prethee down again, shall I find favour Lady? shall at length my true unfeigned penitence get pardon for my harsh unseasoned follies? I'm no more an Atheist, no I doe acknowledge, that dread powerfull Deity, and his all quic'kning heats burn in my breast: oh be not as I was, hard unrelenting; but as I am, be partner of my fires.

ORIANA
Sure we shall have store of Larks, the Skies will not hold up long, I should have look'd as soon for Frost in the dog days, or another Inundation, as hop'd this strange conversion above miracle: let me look upon your Lordship; is your name Gondarino? are you Millains Generall, that great Bugbear bloody-bones, at whose name all women, from the Lady to the Landress, shake like a cold fit?

GONDARINO
Good patience help me, this Fever will inrage my blood again: Madam I'm that man; I'm even he that once did owe unreconcil'd hate to you, and all that bear the name of woman: I'm the man that wrong'd your Honor to the Duke: I am hee that said you were unchast, and prostitute, yet I'm he that dare deny all this.

ORIANA
Your big Nobility is very merry.

GONDARINO
Lady 'tis true that I have wrong'd you thus,
And my contrition is as true as that,
Yet have I found a means to make all good again,
I doe beseech your beautie, not for my self,
My merits are yet in conception,
But for your honors safety and my zeal
Retire a while, while I unsay my self unto the Duke,
And cast out that evill Spirit I have possest him with,
I have a house conveniently private.

ORIANA
Lord, thou hast wrong'd my innocence, but thy confession hath gain'd thee faith.

GONDARINO
By the true honest service, that I owe those eyes
My meaning is as spotless as my faith.

ORIANA
The Duke doubt mine honor? a may judge strangely,
'Twill not be long, before I'll be enlarg'd again.

GONDARINO
A day or two.

ORIANA
Mine own servants shall attend me.

GONDARINO
Your Ladyships command is good.

ORIANA
Look you be true.

[Exit **ORIANA**.

GONDARINO
Else let me lose the hopes my soul aspires to: I will be a scourge to all females in my life, and after my death, the name of Gondarino shall be terrible to the mighty women of the earth; They shall shake at my name, and at the sound of it, their knees shall knock together; And they shall run into Nunneries, for they and I are beyond all hope irreconcilable: for if I could endure an ear with a hole in't, or a pleated lock, or a bare headed Coachman, that sits like a sign where great Ladies are to be sold within; agreement betwixt us, were not to be dispaired of; if I could be but brought to endure to see women, I would have them come all once a week, and kiss me, where Witches doe the devill, in token of homage: I must not live here; I will to the Court, and there pursue my plot; when it hath took, women shall stand in awe, but of my look.

[Exit.

SCÆNA TERTIA

Enter two **INTELLIGENCERS**, discovering treason in the Courtiers words.

1ST INTELLIGENCER
There take your standing, be close and vigilant, here will I set my self, and let him look to his language, a shall know the Duke has more ears in Court than two.

2ND INTELLIGENCER
I'll quote him to a tittle, let him speak wisely, and plainly, and as hidden as a can, or I shall crush him, a shall not scape charracters, though a speak Babel, I shall crush him: we have a Fortune by this service hanging over us, that within this year or two, I hope we shall be called to be examiners, wear politick gowns garded with copper lace, making great faces full of fear and office, our labors may deserve this.

1ST INTELLIGENCER
I hope it shall: why has not many men been raised from this worming trade, first to gain good access to great men, then to have commissions out for search, and lastly, to be worthily nam'd at a great Arraignment: yes, and why not we? They that endeavor well deserve their Fee. Close, close, a comes: mark well, and all goes well.

[Enter **COUNT**, **LAZARELLO**, and his **BOY**.

LAZARELLO
Farewell my hopes, my Anchor now is broken,
Farewell my quondam joys, of which no token
Is now remaining, such is the sad mischance,
Where Lady Fortune leads the slipp'ry dance.

Yet at the length, let me this favour have,
Give me my wishes, or a wished grave.

COUNT
The gods defend so brave and valiant maw,
Should slip into the never satiate jaw
Of black Despair; no, thou shalt live and know
Thy full desires, hunger thy ancient foe,
Shall be subdued; those guts that daily tumble
Through ayr and appetite, shall cease to rumble:
And thou shalt now at length obtain thy dish,
That noble part, the sweet head of a fish.

LAZARELLO
Then am I greater than the Duke.

2ND INTELLIGENCER
There, there's a notable peece of treason, greater than the Duke, mark that.

COUNT
But how, or where, or when this shall be compas'd, is yet out of my reach.

LAZARELLO
I am so truely miserable, that might
I be now knockt oth' head, with all my heart
I would forgive a dog-killer.

COUNT
Yet doe I see through this confusedness some little comfort.

LAZARELLO
The plot my Lord, as er'e you came of a woman, discover.

1ST INTELLIGENCER
Plots, dangerous plots, I will deserve by this most liberally.

COUNT
'Tis from my head again.

LAZARELLO
O that it would stand me, that I might fight, or have some venture for it, that I might be turn'd loose, to
try my fortune amongst the whole frie in a Colledge, or an Inn of Court; or scramble with the prisoners
in the dungeon; nay were it set down in the owter court,
And all the Guard about it in a ring,
With their knives drawn, which were a dismall sight,
And after twenty leisurely were told,
I to be let loose only in my shirt,
To trie the valour, how much of the spoyl,

I would recover from the enemies mouths:
I would accept the challenge.

COUNT
Let it go: hast not thou beene held
To have some wit in the Court, and to make fine jests
Upon country people in progress time, and
Wilt thou lose this opinion, for the cold head of a Fish?
I say, let it goe: I'll help thee to as good a dish of meat.

LAZARELLO
God let me not live, if I doe not wonder,
Men should talk so profanely:
But it is not in the power of loose words,
Of any vain or misbeleeving man,
To make me dare to wrong thy purity.
Shew me but any Lady in the Court,
That hath so full an eye, so sweet a breath,
So soft and white a flesh: this doth not lie
In almond gloves, nor ever hath bin washt
In artificiall baths: no traveller
That hath brought doctor home with him, hath dar'd
With all his waters, powders, Fucusses,
To make thy lovely corps sophisticate.

COUNT
I have it, 'tis now infus'd, be comforted.

LAZARELLO
Can there be that little hope yet left in nature? shall I once more erect up Trophies? Shall I enjoy the sight of my dear Saint, and bless my pallate with the best of creatures, ah good my Lord, by whom I breathe again, shall I receive this Being?

COUNT
Sir I have found by certain calculation, and settled revolution of the stars, the Fish is sent by the Lord Gondarino to his Mercer, now 'tis a growing hope to know where 'tis.

LAZARELLO
O 'tis far above the good of women, the Pathick cannot yield more pleasing titilation.

COUNT
But how to compass it, search, cast about, and bang your brains, Lazarello, thou art too dull and heavy to deserve a blessing.

LAZARELLO
My Lord, I will not be idle; now Lazarello, think, think, think.

COUNT

Yonder's my informer
And his fellow with table books, they nod at me
Upon my life, they have poor Lazarello, that beats
His brains about no such waighty matter, in for
Treason before this—

LAZARELLO
My Lord, what doe you think, if I should shave my self,
Put on midwives apparell, come in with a hand-kercher,
And beg a piece for a great bellied woman, or a sick child?

COUNT
Good, very good.

LAZARELLO
Or corrupt the waiting prentise to betray the reversion.

1ST INTELLIGENCER
There's another point in's plot, corrupt with money; to betray: sure 'tis some Fort a means: mark, have a care.

LAZARELLO
And 'twere the bare vinegar 'tis eaten with, it would in some sort satisfie nature: but might I once attain the dish it self, though I cut out my means through swords and fire, through poison, through any thing that may make good my hopes.

2ND INTELLIGENCER
Thanks to the gods, and our officiousness, the plots discover'd, fire, steel, and poison, burn the Palace, kill the Duke and poison his privie Councell.

COUNT
To the mercers, let me see: how, if before we can attain the means, to make up our acquaintance, the fish be eaten?

LAZARELLO
If it be eaten, here he stands, that is the most dejected, most unfortunate, miserable, accursed, forsaken slave this Province yields: I will not sure outlive it, no I will dye bravely, and like a Roman; and after death, amidst the Elizian shades, I'll meet my love again.

1ST INTELLIGENCER
I will dye bravely, like a Roman: have a care, mark that, when he hath done all, he will kill himself.

COUNT
Will nothing ease your appetite but this?

LAZARELLO
No could the Sea throw up his vastness,
And offer free his best inhabitants: 'twere not so much as a bare temptation to me.

COUNT
If you could be drawn to affect Beef, Venison, or Fowl, 'twould be far the better.

LAZARELLO
I doe beseech your Lordships patience,
I doe confess that in this heat of blood,
I have contemn'd all dull and grosser meats,
But I protest I doe honor a Chine of Beef,
I doe reverence a loyn of Veal,
But good my Lord, give me leave a little to adore this:
But my good Lord, would your Lordship, under color of taking up some silks, goe to the Mercers, I would in all humilitie attend your honor, where we may be invited, if Fortune stand propitious.

COUNT
Sir you shall work me as you please.

LAZARELLO
Let it be suddenly, I doe beseech your Lordship, 'tis now upon the point of dinner time.

COUNT
I am all yours.

[Exeunt **LAZARELLO** and **COUNT**.

1ST INTELLIGENCER
Come let us confer, Imprimis he saith, like a blasphemous villain, he's greater than the Duke, this peppers him, and there were nothing else.

2ND INTELLIGENCER
Then he was naming plots; did you not hear?

1ST INTELLIGENCER
Yes but he fell from that unto discovery, to corrupt by money, and so attain.

2ND INTELLIGENCER
I, I, he meant some Fort, or Cyttadell the Duke hath, his very face betraid his meaning, O he is a very subtile and a dangerous knave, but if he deal a Gods name, we shall worm him.

1ST INTELLIGENCER
But now comes the Stroak, the fatall blow, Fire, Sword and Poyson, O Canibal, thou bloody Canibal.

2ND INTELLIGENCER
2 In. What had become of this poor state, had not we been?

1ST INTELLIGENCER
Faith it had lyen buried in his own ashes; had not a greater hand been in't.

2ND INTELLIGENCER

But note the rascalls resolution, after th'acts done, because he wo'd avoid all fear of torture, and cousen the Law, he wo'd kill himself; was there ever the like danger brought to light in this age? sure we shall merit much, we shall be able to keep two men a peece, and a two handsword between us, we will live in favour of the State, betray our ten or twelve treasons a week, and the people shall fear us: come, to the Lord Lucio, the Sun shall not goe down till he be hang'd.

[Exeunt.

SCÆNA QUARTA

Enter **MERCER**.

MERCER

Look to my shop, and if there come ever a Scholar in black, let him speak with me; we that are shopkeepers in good trade, are so pester'd, that we can scarce pick out an hour for our mornings meditation: and howsoever we are all accounted dull, and common jesting stocks for your gallants; There are some of us doe not deserve it: for, for my own part, I doe begin to be given to my book, I love a scholar with my heart, for questionless there are merveilous things to be done by Art: why Sir, some of them will tell you what is become of horses, and silver spoons, and will make wenches dance naked to their beds: I am yet unmarried, and because some of our neighbours are said to be Cuckolds, I will never marrie without the consent of some of these scholars, that know what will come of it.

[Enter **PANDAR**.

PANDAR

Are you busie Sir?

MERCER

Never to you Sir, nor to any of your coat. Sir is there any
thing to be done by Art, concerning the great heir we talk'd on?

PANDAR

Will she, nill she: she shall come running into my house at the farther corner, in Sa. Marks street, betwixt three and four.

MERCER

Betwixt three and four? she's brave in cloaths, is she not?

PANDAR

O rich! rich! where should I get cloaths to dress her in? Help me invention: Sir, that her running through the street may be less noted, my Art more shown, and your fear to speak with her less, she shall come in a white wastcoat, And—

MERCER

What shall she?

PANDAR
And perhaps torn stockings, she hath left her old wont else.

[Enter **PRENTICE**.

PRENTICE
Sir my Lord Gondarino hath sent you a rare fish head.

MERCER
It comes right, all things sute right with me since I began to love scholars, you shall have it home with you against she come: carrie it to this Gentleman's house.

PANDAR
The fair white house at the farther corner at S. Marks street, make haste, I must leave you too Sir, I have two hours to study; buy a new Accedence, and ply your book, and you shall want nothing that all the scholars in the Town can doe for you.

[Exit **PANDAR**.

MERCER
Heaven prosper both our studies, what a dull slave was I before I fell in love with this learning! not worthy to tread upon the earth, & what fresh hopes it hath put in to me! I doe hope within this twelve-month to be able by Art to serve the Court with silks, and not undoe my self; to trust Knights, and yet get in my money again; to keep my wife brave, and yet she keep no body else so.

[Enter **COUNT** and **LAZARELLO**.

Your Lordship is most honourably welcome in regard of your Nobility; but most especialy in regard of your scholarship: did your Lordship come openly?

COUNT
Sir this cloak keeps me private, besides no man will suspect me to be in the company of this Gentleman, with whom, I will desire you to be acquainted, he may prove a good customer to you.

LAZARELLO
For plain silks and velvets.

MERCER
Are you scholasticall?

LAZARELLO
Something addicted to the Muses.

COUNT
I hope they will not dispute.

MERCER

You have no skill in the black Art.

[Enter a **PRENTICE**.

PRENTICE
Sir yonder's a Gentleman enquires hastily for Count Valore.

COUNT
For me? what is he?

PRENTICE
One of your followers my Lord I think.

COUNT
Let him come in.

MERCER
Shall I talk with you in private Sir?

[Enter a **MESSENGER** with a Letter to the **COUNT**. He reads.

COUNT
Count, come to the Court your business calls you thither, I will goe, farewell Sir, I will see your silks some
other time: Farewell Lazarillo.

MERCER
Will not your Lordship take a piece of Beef with me?

COUNT
Sir I have greater business than eating; I will leave this
Gentleman with you.

[Exeunt **COUNT** & **MESSENGER**.

LAZARELLO
No, no, no, no: now doe I feel that strain'd struggling within me, that I think I could prophesie.

MERCER
The Gentleman is meditating.

LAZARELLO
Hunger, valour, love, ambition are alike pleasing, and let our Philosophers say what they will, are one
kind of heat, only hunger is the safest: ambition is apt to fall; love and valour are not free from dangers;
only hunger, begotten of some old limber Courtier, in pan'de hose, and nurs'd by an Attourneys wife;
now so thriven, that he need not fear to be of the great Turks guard: is so free from all quarrels and
dangers, so full of hopes, joyes, and ticklings, that my life is not so dear to me as his acquaintance.

[Enter Lazarello's **BOY**.

BOY

Sir the Fish head is gone.

LAZARELLO

Then be thou henceforth dumb, with thy ill-boding voice.
Farewell Millain, farewell Noble Duke,
Farewell my fellow Courtiers all, with whom,
I have of yore made many a scrambling meal
In corners, behind Arasses, on stairs;
And in the action oftentimes have spoil'd,
Our Doublets and our Hose with liquid stuff:
Farewell you lusty Archers of the Guard,
To whom I now doe give the bucklers up,
And never more with any of your coat
Will eat for wagers, now you happy be,
When this shall light upon you, think on me:
You sewers, carvers, ushers of the court
Sirnamed gentle for your fair demean,
Here I doe take of you my last farewell,
May you stand stifly in your proper places,
And execute your offices aright.
Farewell you Maidens, with your mother eke,
Farewell you courtly Chaplains that be there
All good attend you, may you never more
Marry your Patrons Ladys wayting-woman,
But may you raised be by this my fall
May Lazarillo suffer for you all.

MERCER

Sir I was hearkning to you.

LAZARELLO

I will hear nothing, I will break my knife, the Ensign of my former happy state, knock out my teeth, have them hung at a Barbers, and enter into Religion.

BOY

Why Sir, I think I know whither it is gone.

LAZARELLO

See the rashness of man in his nature, whither? I do unsay all that I have said, go on, go on: Boy, I humble my self and follow thee; Farewell Sir.

MERCER

Not so Sir, you shall take a piece of Beef with me.

LAZARELLO

I cannot stay.

MERCER
By my fay but you shall Sir, in regard of your love to learning, and your skill in the black Art.

LAZARELLO
I do hate learning, and I have no skill in the black Art,
I would I had.

MERCER
Why your desire is sufficient to me, you shall stay.

LAZARELLO
The most horrible and detested curses that can be imagined, light upon all the professors of that Art;
may they be drunk, and when they goe to conjure, and reel in the Circle, may the spirits by them rais'd,
tear 'em in pieces, and hang their quarters on old broken walls and Steeple tops.

MERCER
This speech of yours, shews you to have some skill in the Science, wherefore in civilitie, I may not suffer
you to depart empty.

LAZARELLO
My stomach is up, I cannot endure it, I will fight in this quarrell as soon as for my Prince.

[Draws his Rapier.

[Exeunt **OMNES**.

Room, make way:
Hunger commands, my valour must obey.

ACTUS QUARTUS

SCÆNA PRIMA

Enter **COUNT** and **ARRIGO**.

COUNT
Is the Duke private?

ARRIGO
He is alone, but I think your Lordship may enter.

[Exit **COUNT**.

[Enter **GONDARINO**.

GONDARINO
Who's with the Duke?

ARRIGO
The Count is new gone in; but the Duke will come forth,
before you can be weary of waiting.

GONDARINO
I will attend him here.

ARRIGO
I must wait without the door.

[Exit **ARRIGO**.

GONDARINO
Doth he hope to clear his Sister? she will come no more to my house, to laugh at me: I have sent her to a habitation, where when she shall be seen, it will set a gloss upon her name; yet upon my soul I have bestow'd her amongst the purest hearted creatures of her sex, and the freest from dissimulation; for their deeds are all alike, only they dare speak, what the rest think: the women of this age, if there be any degrees of comparison amongst their sex, are worse than those of former times; for I have read of women, of that truth, spirit, and constancy, that were they now living, I should endure to see them: but I fear the writers of the time belied them, for how familiar a thing is it with the Poets of our age, to extoll their whores, which they call Mistresses, with heavenly praises! but I thank their furies, and their craz'd brains, beyond belief: nay, how many that would fain seem serious, have dedicated grave Works to Ladies, toothless, hollow-ey'd, their hair shedding, purple fac'd, their nails apparently coming off; and the bridges of their noses broken down, and have call'd them the choice handy works of nature, the patterns of perfection, and the wonderment of Women. Our Women begin to swarm like Bees in Summer: as I came hither, there was no pair of stairs, no entry, no lobby, but was pestred with them: methinks there might be some course taken to destroy them.

[Enter **ARRIGO**, and an old deaf countrey **GENTLEWOMAN**, suitor to the Duke.

ARRIGO
I do accept your money, walk here, and when the Duke comes out, you shall have fit opportunity to deliver your petition to him.

GENTLEWOMAN
I thank you heartily, I pray you who's he that walks there?

ARRIGO
A Lord, and a Soldier, one in good favour with the Duke; if you could get him to deliver your Petition—

GENTLEWOMAN
What do you say, Sir?

ARRIGO
If you could get him to deliver your petition for you, or to second you, 'twere sure.

GENTLEWOMAN
I hope I shall live to requite your kindness.

ARRIGO
You have already.

[Exit **ARRIGO**.

GENTLEWOMAN
May it please your Lordship—

GONDARINO
No, no.

GENTLEWOMAN
To consider the estate—

GONDARINO
No.

GENTLEWOMAN
Of a poor oppressed countrey Gentlewoman.

GONDARINO
No, it doth not please my Lordship.

GENTLEWOMAN
First and formost, I have had great injury, then I have been brought up to the Town three times.

GONDARINO
A pox on him, that brought thee to the Town.

GENTLEWOMAN
I thank your good Lordship heartily; though I cannot hear well, I know it grieves you; and here we have been delaid, and sent down again, and fetch'd up again, and sent down again, to my great charge: and now at last they have fetch'd me up, and five of my daughters—

GONDARINO
Enough to damn five worlds.

GENTLEWOMAN
Handsome young women, though I say it, they are all without, if it please your Lordship I'll call them in.

GONDARINO
Five Women! how many of my sences should I have left me
then? call in five Devils first.
No, I will rather walk with thee alone,

And hear thy tedious tale of injury,
And give thee answers; whisper in thine ear,
And make thee understand through thy French hood:
And all this with tame patience.

GENTLEWOMAN
I see your Lordship does believe, that they are without, and I perceive you are much mov'd at our injury: here's a paper will tell you more.

GONDARINO
Away.

GENTLEWOMAN
It may be you had rather hear me tell it viva voce, as they say.

GONDARINO
Oh no, no, no, no, I have heard it before.

GENTLEWOMAN
Then you have heard of enough injury, for a poor Gentlewoman to receive.

GONDARINO
Never, never, but that it troubles my conscience, to wish any good to these women; I could afford them to be valiant, and able, that it might be no disgrace for a Soldier to beat them.

GENTLEWOMAN
I hope your Lordship will deliver my petition to his grace, and you may tell him withal—

GONDARINO
What? I will deliver any thing against my self, to be rid on thee.

GENTLEWOMAN
That yesterday about three a clock in the after noon, I met my adversary.

GONDARINO
Give me thy paper, he can abide no long tales.

GENTLEWOMAN
'Tis very short my Lord, and I demanding of him—

GONDARINO
I'll tell him that shall serve thy turn.

GENTLEWOMAN
How?

GONDARINO

I'll tell him that shall serve thy turn, begone: man never doth remember how great his offences are, till he do meet with one of you, that plagues him for them: why should Women only above all other creatures that were created for the benefit of man, have the use of speech? or why should any deed of theirs, done by their fleshly appetites, be disgraceful to their owners? nay, why should not an act done by any beast I keep, against my consent, disparage me as much as that of theirs?

GENTLEWOMAN
Here's some few Angels for your Lordship.

GONDARINO
Again? yet more torments?

GENTLEWOMAN
Indeed you shall have them.

GONDARINO
Keep off.

GENTLEWOMAN
A small gratuity for your kindness.

GONDARINO
Hold away.

GENTLEWOMAN
Why then I thank your Lordship, I'll gather them up again, and I'll be sworn, it is the first money that was refus'd since I came to the Court.

GONDARINO
What can she devise to say more?

GENTLEWOMAN
Truly I would have willingly parted with them to your Lordship.

GONDARINO
I believe it, I believe it.

GENTLEWOMAN
But since it is thus—

GONDARINO
More yet.

GENTLEWOMAN
I will attend without, and expect an answer.

GONDARINO

Do, begone, and thou shalt expect, and have any thing, thou shalt have thy answer from him; and he were best to give thee a good one at first, for thy deaf importunity, will conquer him too, in the end.

GENTLEWOMAN
Gentlew. God bless your Lordship, and all that favour a poor distressed countrey Gentlewoman.

[Exit **GENTLEWOMAN.**

GONDARINO
All the diseases of man light upon them that doe, and upon me when I do. A week of such days, would either make me stark mad or tame me: yonder other woman that I have sure enough, shall answer for thy sins: dare they incense me still, I will make them fear as much to be ignorant of me and my moods, as men are to be ignorant of the law they live under. Who's there? My bloud grew cold, I began to fear my Suiters return; 'tis the Duke.

[Enter the **DUKE** and the **COUNT.**

COUNT
I know her chaste, though she be young and free,
And is not of that forc'd behaviour
That many others are, and that this Lord,
Out of the boundless malice to the sex,
Hath thrown this scandal on her.

GONDARINO
Fortune befriended me against my Will, with this good old countrey gentlewoman; I beseech your grace, to view favourably the petition of a wronged Gentlewoman.

DUKE
What Gondarino, are you become a petitioner for your enemies?

GONDARINO
My Lord, they are no enemies of mine, I confess, the better to cover my deeds, which sometimes were loose enough, I pretended it, as it is wisdom, to keep close our incontinence, but since you have discover'd me, I will no more put on that vizard, but will as freely open all my thoughts to you, as to my Confessor.

DUKE
What say you to this?

COUNT
He that confesses he did once dissemble,
I'll never trust his words: can you imagine
A Maid, whose beauty could not suffer her
To live thus long untempted, by the noblest,
Richest, and cunningst Masters in that Art
And yet hath ever held a fair repute;
Could in one morning, and by him be brought,

To forget all her virtue, and turn whore?

GONDARINO
I would I had some other talk in hand,
Than to accuse a Sister to her Brother:
Nor do I mean it for a publick scandal,
Unless by urging me you make it so.

DUKE
I will read this at better leisure: Gondarino, where is the Lady?

COUNT
At his house.

GONDARINO
No, she is departed thence.

COUNT
Whither?

GONDARINO
Urge it not thus, or let me be excus'd,
If what I speak betray her chastity,
And both increase my sorrow, and your own?

COUNT
Fear me not so, if she deserve the fame
Which she hath gotten, I would have it publisht,
Brand her my self, and whip her through the City:
I wish those of my bloud that doe offend,
Should be more strictly punisht, than my foes.
Let it be prov'd.

DUKE
Gondarino, thou shalt prove it, or suffer worse than she should do.

GONDARINO
Then pardon me, if I betray the faults
Of one, I love more dearly than my self,
Since opening hers, I shall betray mine own:
But I will bring you where she now intends
Not to be virtuous: pride and wantonness,
That are true friends indeed, though not in shew,
Have entr'd on her heart, there she doth bathe,
And sleek her hair, and practise cunning looks
To entertain me with; and hath her thoughts
As full of lust, as ever you did think
Them full of modesty.

DUKE
Gondarino, lead on, we'll follow thee.

[Exeunt.

SCÆNA SECUNDA

Enter **PANDAR**.

PANDAR
Here hope I to meet my Citizen, and here hopes he to meet his Scholar; I am sure I am grave enough, to his eyes, and knave enough to deceive him: I am believ'd to conjure, raise storms, and devils, by whose power I can do wonders; let him believe so still, belief hurts no man; I have an honest black cloak, for my knavery, and a general pardon for his foolery, from this present day, till the day of his breaking. Is't not a misery, and the greatest of our age, to see a handsome, young, fair enough, and well mounted wench, humble her self, in an old stammel petticoat, standing possest of no more fringe, than the street can allow her: her upper parts so poor and wanting, that ye may see her bones through her bodies: shoes she would have, if her Captain were come over, and is content the while to devote her self to antient slippers. These premises well considered, Gentlemen, will move, they make me melt I promise ye, they stirr me much: and wer't not for my smooth, soft, silken Citizen, I would quit this transitory Trade, get me an everlasting Robe, sear up my conscience, and turn Serjeant. But here he comes, is mine as good as prize: Sir Pandarus be my speed, ye are most fitly met Sir.

[Enter **MERCER**.

MERCER
And you as well encount'red, what of this heir? hath your
Books been propitious?

PANDAR
Sir, 'tis done, she's come, she's in my house, make your self apt for Courtship, stroke up your stockings, loose not an inch of your legs goodness; I am sure ye wear socks.

MERCER
There your Books fail ye Sir, in truth I wear no socks.

PANDAR
I would you had, Sir, it were the sweeter grace for your legs; get on your Gloves, are they perfum'd?

MERCER
A pretty wash I'll assure you.

PANDAR
'Twill serve: your offers must be full of bounty, Velvets to furnish a Gown, Silks for Peticoats and Foreparts, Shag for lining; forget not some pretty Jewel to fasten, after some little compliment: if she

deny this courtesie, double your bounties, be not wanting in abundance, fulness of gifts, link'd with a pleasing tongue, will win an Anchorite. Sir, ye are my friend, and friend to all that professes good Letters; I must not use this office else, it fits not for a Scholar, and a Gentleman: those stockings are of Naples, they are silk?

MERCER
Ye are again beside your Text, Sir, they're of the best of
Wooll, and they cleeped Jersey.

PANDAR
Sure they are very dear.

MERCER
Nine shillings, by my love to learning.

PANDAR
Pardon my judgement, we Scholars use no other objects, but our Books.

MERCER
There is one thing entomb'd in that grave breast, that makes me equally admire it with your Scholarship.

PANDAR
Sir; but that in modesty I am bound not to affect mine own commendation, I would enquire it of you.

MERCER
Sure you are very honest; and yet ye have a kind of modest fear to shew it: do not deny it, that face of yours is a worthy, learned modest face.

PANDAR
Sir, I can blush.

MERCER
Virtue and grace are always pair'd together: but I will leave to stirr your bloud Sir, and now to our business.

PANDAR
Forget not my instructions.

MERCER
I apprehend ye Sir, I will gather my self together with my best phrases, and so I shall discourse in some sort takingly.

PANDAR
This was well worded Sir, and like a Scholar.

MERCER
The Muses favour me as my intents are virtuous;
Sir, ye shall be my Tutor, 'tis never too late Sir, to love

Learning.
When I can once speak true Latine—

PANDAR
What do you intend Sir?

MERCER
Marry I will then begger all your bawdy Writers, and undertake, at the peril of my own invention, all Pageants, Poesies for Chimneys, Speeches for the Dukes entertainment, whensoever and whatsoever; nay I will build, at mine own charge, an Hospital, to which shall retire all diseased opinions, all broken Poets, all Prose-men that are fall'n from small sence, to meer Letters; and it shall be lawful for a Lawyer, if he be a civil man, though he have undone others and himself by the language, to retire to this poor life, and learn to be honest.

PANDAR
Sir, ye are very good, and very charitable: ye are a true pattern for the City Sir.

MERCER
Sir, I doe know sufficiently, their Shop-books cannot save them, there is a farther end—

PANDAR
Pand. Oh Sir, much may be done by manuscript.

MERCER
I do confess it Sir, provided still they be Canonical, and have some worthy hands set to 'um for probation: but we forget our selves.

PANDAR
Sir, enter when you please, and all good language tip your tongue.

MERCER
All that love Learning pray for my good success.

[Exit **MERCER**.

SCÆNA TERTIA

Enter **LAZARELLO** and his **BOY**.

LAZARELLO
Boy, whereabouts are we?

BOY
Sir, by all tokens this is the house, bawdy I am sure, by the broken windows, the Fish head is within; if ye dare venture, here you may surprize it.

LAZARELLO

The misery of man may fitly be compar'd to a Didapper, who when she is under water, past our sight, and indeed can seem no more to us, rises again; shakes but her self, and is the same she was, so is it still with transitory man, this day: oh but an hour since, and I was mighty, mighty in knowledge, mighty in my hopes, mighty in blessed means, and was so truly happy, that I durst have said, live Lazarello, and be satisfied: but now—

BOY

Sir, ye are yet afloat, and may recover, be not your own wreck, here lies the harbor, goe in and ride at ease.

LAZARELLO

Boy, I am receiv'd to be a Gentleman, a Courtier, and a man of action, modest, and wise, and be it spoken with thy reverence, Child, abounding virtuous; and wouldst thou have a man of these choise habits, covet the cover of a bawdy-house? yet if I goe not in, I am but—

BOY

But what Sir?

LAZARELLO

Dust boy, but dust, and my soul unsatisfied shall haunt the keepers of my blessed Saint, and I will appear.

BOY

An ass to all men; Sir, these are no means to stay your appetite, you must resolve to enter.

LAZARELLO

Were not the house subject to Martial Law—

BOY

If that be all, Sir, ye may enter, for ye can know nothing here that the Court is ignorant of, only the more eyes shall look upon you, for there they wink one at anothers faults.

LAZARELLO

If I doe not.

BOY

Then ye must beat fairly back again, fall to your physical mess of porridge, and the twice sack'd carkass of a Capon: Fortune may favour you so much, to send the bread to it: but it's a mere venture, and money may be put out upon it.

LAZARELLO

I will go in and live; pretend some love to the Gentlewoman, screw my self in affection, and so be satisfied.

PANDAR

This Fly is caught, is mash'd already, I will suck him, and lay him by.

BOY

Muffle your self in your cloak by any means, 'tis a receiv'd thing among gallants, to walk to their leachery, as though they had the rheum, 'twas well you brought not your horse.

LAZARELLO

Why Boy?

BOY

Faith Sir, 'tis the fashion of our Gentry, to have their horses wait at door like men, while the beasts their Masters, are within at rack and manger, 'twould have discover'd much.

LAZARELLO

I will lay by these habits, forms, and grave respects of what I am, and be my self; only my appetite, my fire, my soul, my being, my dear appetite shall go along with me, arm'd with whose strength, I fearless will attempt the greatest danger dare oppose my fury: I am resolv'd where ever that thou art, most sacred dish, hid from unhallow'd eyes, to find thee out.
Be'st thou in Hell, rap't by Proserpina,
To be a rival in black Pluto's love;
Or mov'st thou in the heavens, a form Divine:
Lashing the lazie Sphears,
Or if thou be'st return'd to thy first Being,
Thy mother Sea, there will I seek thee forth.
Earth, Air, nor Fire,
Nor the black shades below shall bar my sight
So daring is my powerful appetite.

BOY

Sir, you may save this long voyage, and take a shorter cut: you have forgot your self, the fish head's here, your own imaginations have made you mad.

LAZARELLO

Term it a jealous fury, good my boy.

BOY

Faith Sir term it what you will, you must use other terms ere you can get it.

LAZARELLO

The looks of my sweet love are fair,
Fresh and feeding as the air.

BOY

Sir, you forget your self.

LAZARELLO

Was never seen so rare a head,
Of any Fish alive or dead.

BOY

Good Sir remember: this is the house, Sir.

LAZARELLO
Cursed be he that dare not venture.

BOY
Pity your self, Sir, and leave this fury.

LAZARELLO
For such a prize, and so I enter.

[Exit **LAZARELLO** and **BOY**.

PANDAR
Dun's i'th' mire, get out again how he can:
My honest gallant, I'll shew you one trick more
Than e'er the fool your father dream'd of yet.
Madona Julia?

[Enter Madona **JULIA**, a Whore.

JULIA
What news my sweet rogue, my dear sins-broker, what? Good news?

PANDAR
There is a kind of ignorant thing,
Much like a Courtier, now gone in.

JULIA
Is he gallant?

PANDAR
He shines not very gloriously, nor does he wear one skin perfum'd to keep the other sweet; his coat is not in Or, nor does the world run yet on wheels with him; he's rich enough, and has a small thing follows him, like to a boat tyed to a tall ships tail: give him entertainment, be light, and flashing like a Meteor, hug him about the neck, give him a kiss, and lisping cry, good Sir; and he's thine own, as fast as he were tied to thine arms by Indentures.

JULIA
I dare doe more than this, if he be o'th' true Court cut; I'll take him out a lesson worth the Learning: but we are but their Apes; what's he worth?

PANDAR
Be he rich, or poor; if he will take thee with him, thou maist use thy trade free from Constables, and Marshals: who hath been here since I went out?

JULIA

There is a Gentlewoman sent hither by a Lord, she's a piece of dainty stuff my rogue, smooth and soft, as new Sattin; she was never gumm'd yet boy, nor fretted.

PANDAR
Where lies she?

JULIA
She lies above, towards the street, not to be spoke with, but by the Lord that sent her, or some from him, we have in charge from his servants.

[Enter **LAZARELLO**.

PANDAR
Peace, he comes out again upon discovery; up with all your Canvas, hale him in; and when thou hast done, clap him aboard bravely, my valiant Pinnace.

JULIA
Begone, I shall doe reason with him.

LAZARELLO
Are you the special beauty of this house?

JULIA
Sir, you have given it a more special regard by your good language, than these black brows can merit.

LAZARELLO
Lady, you are fair.

JULIA
Fair Sir? I thank ye; all the poor means I have left to be thought grateful, is but a kiss, and ye shall have it Sir.

LAZARELLO
Ye have a very moving lip.

JULIA
Prove it again Sir, it may be your sense was set too high, and so over-wrought it self.

LAZARELLO
'Tis still the same: how far may ye hold the time to be spent Lady?

JULIA
Four a clock, Sir.

LAZARELLO
I have not eat to day.

JULIA

You will have the better stomach to your supper; in the mean time I'll feed you with delight.

LAZARELLO
'Tis not so good upon an empty stomach: if it might be without the trouble of your house, I would eat?

JULIA
Sir, we can have a Capon ready.

LAZARELLO
The day?

JULIA
'Tis Friday, Sir.

LAZARELLO
I do eat little flesh upon these days.

JULIA
Come sweet, ye shall not think on meat; I'll drown it with a better appetite.

LAZARELLO
I feel it work more strangely, I must eat.

JULIA
'Tis now too late to send; I say ye shall not think on meat: if ye do, by this kiss I'll be angry.

LAZARELLO
I could be far more sprightful, had I eaten, and more lasting.

JULIA
What will you have Sir? name but the Fish, my Maid shall bring it, if it may be got.

LAZARELLO
Methinks your house should not be so unfurnish'd, as not to have some pretty modicum.

JULIA
It is so now: but you'd ye stay till supper?

LAZARELLO
Sure I have offended highly, and much, and my inflictions makes it manifest, I will retire henceforth, and keep my chamber, live privately, and dye forgotten.

JULIA
Sir, I must crave your pardon, I had forgot my self; I have a dish of meat within, and it is fish; I think this Dukedom holds not a daintier: 'tis an Umbranoes head.

LAZARELLO
Lady, this kiss is yours, and this.

JULIA

Hoe! within there! cover the board, and set the Fish head on it.

LAZARELLO

Now am I so truly happy, so much above all fate and fortune, that I should despise that man, durst say, remember Lazarello, thou art mortal.

[Enter **INTELLIGENCERS** with a **GUARD**.

2ND INTELLIGENCER

This is the villain, lay hands on him.

LAZARELLO

Gentlemen, why am I thus intreated? what is the nature of my crime?

2ND INTELLIGENCER

Sir, though you have carried it a great while privately, and (as you think) well; yet we have seen you Sir, and we do know thee Lazarello, for a Traitor.

LAZARELLO

The gods defend our Duke.

2ND INTELLIGENCER

Amen, Sir, Sir, this cannot save that stiff neck from the halter.

JULIA

Gentlemen, I am glad you have discover'd him, he should not have eaten under my roof for twenty pounds; and surely I did not like him, when he call'd for Fish.

LAZARELLO

My friends, will ye let
me have that little favour—

1ST INTELLIGENCER

Sir, ye shall have Law, and nothing else.

LAZARELLO

To let me stay the eating of a bit or two, for I protest I am yet fasting.

JULIA

I'll have no Traitor come within my house.

LAZARELLO

Now could I wish my self I had been a Traitor, I have strength enough for to endure it, had I but patience: Man thou art but grass, thou art a bubble, and thou must perish.
Then lead along, I am prepar'd for all:
Since I have lost my hopes, welcome my fall.

2ND INTELLIGENCER
Away Sir.

LAZARELLO
As thou hast hope of man, stay but this dish this two hours, I doubt not but I shall be discharged: by this light I will marry thee.

JULIA
You shall marry me first then.

LAZARELLO
I do contract my self unto thee now, before these Gentlemen.

JULIA
I'll preserve it till you be hang'd or quitted.

LAZARELLO
Thanks, thanks.

2ND INTELLIGENCER
Away, away, you shall thank her at the gallows.

LAZARELLO
Adieu, adieu.

[Exeunt **LAZARELLO, 2ND INTELLIGENCER** and **GUARD.**

JULIA
If he live I'll have him, if he be hang'd, there's no loss in it.

[Exit.

[Enter **ORIANA** and her **WAITING WOMAN**, looking out at a window.

ORIANA
Hast thou provided one to bear my Letter to my brother?

WAITING WOMAN
I have enquir'd, but they of the house will suffer no Letter nor message to be carried from you, but such as the Lord Gondarino shall be acquainted with: truly Madam I suspect the house to be no better than it should be.

ORIANA
What dost thou doubt?

WAITING WOMAN
Faith I am loth to tell it, Madam.

ORIANA
Out with it, 'tis not true modesty to fear to speak that thou dost think.

WAITING WOMAN
I think it be one of these same Bawdy houses.

ORIANA
'Tis no matter wench, we are warm in it, keep thou thy mind pure, and upon my word, that name will do thee no hurt: I cannot force my self yet to fear any thing; when I do get out, I'll have another encounter with my Woman-Hater. Here will I sit. I may get sight of some of my friends, it must needs be a comfort to them to see me here.

[Enter **DUKE**, **GONDARINO**, **COUNT**, **ARRIGO**.

GONDARINO
Are we all sufficiently disguis'd? for this house where she attends me, is not to be visited in our own shapes.

DUKE
We are not our selves.

ARRIGO
I know the house to be sinful enough, yet I have been heretofore, and durst now, but for discovering of you, appear here in my own likeness.

DUKE
Where's Lucio?

ARRIGO
My Lord, he said the affairs of the Common-wealth would not suffer him to attend always.

DUKE
Some great ones questionless that he will handle.

COUNT
Come, let us enter.

GONDARINO
See how Fortune strives to revenge my quarrel upon these women, she's in the window, were it not to undoe her, I should not look upon her.

DUKE
Lead us Gondarino.

GONDARINO
Stay; since you force me to display my shame,
Look there, and you my Lord, know you that face?

DUKE

Is't she?

COUNT

It is.

GONDARINO

'Tis she, whose greatest virtue ever was
Dissimulation; she that still hath strove
More to sin cunningly, than to avoid it:
She that hath ever sought to be accounted
Most virtuous, when she did deserve most scandal:
'Tis she that itches now, and in the height
Of her intemperate thoughts, with greedy eyes
Expects my coming to allay her Lust:
Leave her; forget she's thy sister.

COUNT

Stay, stay.

DUKE

I am as full of this, as thou canst be,
The memory of this will easily
Hereafter stay my loose and wandring thoughts
From any Woman.

COUNT

This will not down with me, I dare not trust this fellow.

DUKE

Leave her here, that only shall be her punishment, never to be fetcht from hence; but let her use her trade to get her living.

COUNT

Stay good my Lord, I do believe all this, as great men as I, have had known whores to their Sisters, and have laught at it: I would fain hear how she talks, since she grew thus light: will your grace make him shew himself to her, as if he were now come to satisfie her longing? whilst we, unseen of her, over-hear her wantonness, let's make our best of it now, we shall have good mirth.

DUKE

Do it Gondarino.

GONDARINO

I must; fortune assist me but this once.

COUNT

Here we shall stand unseen, and near enough.

GONDARINO
Madam, Oriana.

ORIANA
Who's that? oh! my Lord?

GONDARINO
Shall I come up?

ORIANA
Oh you are merry, shall I come down?

GONDARINO
It is better there.

ORIANA
What is the confession of the lye you made to the Duke, which I scarce believe, yet you had impudence enough to do? did it not gain you so much faith with me, as that I was willing to be at your Lordships bestowing, till you had recover'd my credit, and confest your self a lyar, as you pretended to do? I confess I began to fear you, and desir'd to be out of your house, but your own followers forc'd me hither.

GONDARINO
'Tis well suspected, dissemble still, for there are some may hear us.

ORIANA
More tricks yet, my Lord? what house this is I know not, I only know my self: it were a great conquest, if you could fasten a scandal upon me: 'faith my Lord, give me leave to write to my brother?

DUKE
Come down.

COUNT
Come down.

ARRIGO
If it please your Grace, there's a back door.

COUNT
Come meet us there then.

DUKE
It seems you are acquainted with the house.

ARRIGO
I have been in it.

GONDARINO
She saw you and dissembled.

DUKE
Sir, we shall know that better.

GONDARINO
Bring me unto her, if I prove her not
To be a strumpet, let me be contemn'd
Of all her sex.

[Exeunt.

Enter **LUCIO**.

LUCIO
Now whilst the young Duke follows his delights,
We that do mean to practise in the State,
Must pick our times, and set our faces in,
And nod our heads as it may prove most fit
For the main good of the dear Common-wealth:
Who's within there?

[Enter a **SERVANT**.

SERVANT
My Lord?

LUCIO
Secretary, fetch the Gown I use to read Petitions in, and the Standish I answer French Letters with: and call in the Gentleman that attends:

[Exit **SERVANT**.

Little know they that do not deal in State,
How many things there are to be observ'd,
Which seem but little; yet by one of us
(Whose brains do wind about the Common-wealth)
Neglected, cracks our credits utterly.

[Enter **GENTLEMAN** and a **SERVANT**.

Sir, but that I do presume upon your secresie, I would not have appear'd to you thus ignorantly attir'd without a tooth-pick in a ribbond, or a Ring in my bandstrings.

GENTLEMAN
Your Lordship sent for me?

LUCIO
I did: Sir, your long practice in the State, under a great man, hath led you to much experience.

GENTLEMAN
My Lord.

LUCIO
Suffer not your modesty to excuse it: in short, and in private, I desire your direction, I take my study already to be furnisht after a grave and wise method.

GENTLEMAN
What will this Lord do?

LUCIO
My Book-strings are sutable, and of a reaching colour.

GENTLEMAN
How's this?

LUCIO
My Standish of Wood, strange and sweet, and my fore-flap hangs in the right place, and as near Machiavel's, as can be gathered by tradition.

GENTLEMAN
Are there such men as will say nothing abroad, and play the fools in their Lodgings? this Lord must be followed: and hath your Lordship some new made words to scatter in your speeches in publick, to gain note, that the hearers may carry them away, and dispute of them at dinner?

LUCIO
I have Sir: and besides, my several Gowns and Caps agreeable to my several occasions.

GENTLEMAN
'Tis well, and you have learn'd to write a bad hand, that the Readers may take pains for it.

LUCIO
Yes Sir, and I give out I have the palsie.

GENTLEMAN
Good, 'twere better though, if you had it: your Lordship hath a Secretary, that can write fair, when you purpose to be understood.

LUCIO

'Faith Sir I have one, there he stands, he hath been my Secretary these seven years, but he hath forgotten to write.

GENTLEMAN
If he can make a writing face, it is not amiss, so he keep his own counsel: your Lordship hath no hope of the Gout?

LUCIO
Uh, little Sir, since the pain in my right foot left me.

GENTLEMAN
'Twill be some scandal to your wisdom, though I see your Lordship knows enough in publick business.

LUCIO
I am not imploy'd (though to my desert) in occasions foreign, nor frequented for matters domestical.

GENTLEMAN
Not frequented? what course takes your Lordship?

LUCIO
The readiest way, my door stands wide, my Secretary knows I am not denied to any.

GENTLEMAN
In this give me leave your Lordship is out of the way: make a back door to let out Intelligencers; seem to be ever busie, and put your door under keepers, and you shall have a troop of Clients sweating to come at you.

LUCIO
I have a back door already, I will henceforth be busie,
Secretary, run and keep the door.

[Exit **SECRETARY**.

GENTLEMAN
This will fetch 'um?

LUCIO
I hope so.

[Enter **SECRETARY**.

SECRETARY
My Lord, there are some require access to you, about weighty affairs of State.

LUCIO
Already?

GENTLEMAN

I told you so.

LUCIO
How weighty is the business?

SECRETARY
Treason my Lord.

LUCIO
Sir, my debts to you for this are great.

GENTLEMAN
I will leave your Lordship now.

LUCIO
Sir, my death must be suddain, if I requite you not: at the back door good Sir.

GENTLEMAN
I will be your Lordships Intelligencer for once.

[Exit **GENTLEMAN**.

[Enter **SECRETARY**.

SECRETARY
My Lord.

LUCIO
Let 'em in, and say I am at my study.

[Enter **LAZARELLO**, and **TWO INTELLIGENCERS**, **LUCIO** being at his study.

1ST INTELLIGENCER
Where is your Lord?

SECRETARY
At his study, but he will have you brought in.

LAZARELLO
Why Gentlemen, what will you charge me withal?

2ND INTELLIGENCER
Treason, horrible treason, I hope to have the leading of thee to prison, and prick thee on i'th' arse with a Halbert: to have him hang'd that salutes thee, and call all those in question that spit not upon thee.

LAZARELLO
My thred is spun, yet might I but call for this dish of meat at the gallows, instead of a Psalm, it were to be endur'd: the Curtain opens, now my end draws on.

[**SECRETARY** draws the Curtain.

LUCIO
Gentlemen, I am not empty of weighty occasions at this time;
I pray you your business.

1ST INTELLIGENCER
My Lord, I think we have discover'd one of the most bloudy
Traitors, that ever the world held.

LUCIO
Signior Lazarillo, I am glad ye are one of this discovery, give me your hand.

2ND INTELLIGENCER
My Lord, that is the Traitor.

LUCIO
Keep him off, I would not for my whole estate have touchd him.

LAZARELLO
My Lord.

LUCIO
Peace Sir, I know the devil is at your tongue's end, to furnish you with speeches: what are the particulars
you charge him with?

[They deliver a paper to **LUCIO**, who reads.

BOTH INTELLIGENCERS
We have conferr'd our Notes, and have extracted that, which we will justifie upon our oaths.

LUCIO
That he would be greater than the Duke, that he had cast plots for this, and meant to corrupt some to
betray him, that he would burn the City, kill the Duke, and poison the Privy Council; and lastly kill
himself. Though thou deserv'st justly to be hang'd with silence, yet I allow thee to speak, be short.

LAZARELLO
My Lord, so may my greatest wish succeed,
So may I live, and compass what I seek,
As I had never treason in my thoughts,
Nor ever did conspire the overthrow
Of any creatures but of brutish beasts,
Fowls, Fishes, and such other humane food,
As is provided for the good of man.
If stealing Custards, Tarts, and Florentines
By some late Statute be created Treason;
How many fellow-Courtiers can I bring,

Whose long attendance and experience,
Hath made them deeper in the plot than I?

LUCIO
Peace, such hath ever been the clemency of my gracious Master the Duke, in all his proceedings, that I had thought, and thought I had thought rightly; that malice would long e'r this have hid her self in her Den, and have turn'd her own sting against her own heart: but I well now perceive, that so forward is the disposition of a deprav'd nature, that it doth not only seek revenge, where it hath receiv'd injury, but many times thirst after their destruction, where it hath met with benefits.

LAZARELLO
But my good Lord—

2ND INTELLIGENCER
Let's gag him.

LUCIO
Peace again, but many times thirst after destruction, where it hath met with benefits; there I left: Such, and no better are the business that we have now in hand.

1ST INTELLIGENCER
He's excellently spoken.

2ND INTELLIGENCER
He'll wind a Traitor I warrant him.

LUCIO
But surely methinks, setting aside the touch of conscience, and all other inward convulsions.

2ND INTELLIGENCER
He'll be hang'd, I know by that word.

LAZARELLO
Your Lordship may consider—

LUCIO
Hold thy peace: thou canst not answer this speech: no
Traitor can answer it: but because you cannot answer this speech,
I take it you have confess'd the Treason.

1ST INTELLIGENCER
The Count Valore was the first that discover'd him, and can witness it; but he left the matter to your Lordship's grave consideration.

LUCIO
I thank his Lordship, carry him away speedily to the Duke.

LAZARELLO

Now Lazarillo thou art tumbl'd down
The hill of fortune, with a violent arm;
All plagues that can be, Famine, and the Sword
Will light upon thee, black despair will boil
In thy despairing breast, no comfort by,
Thy friends far off, thy enemies are nigh.

LUCIO
Away with him, I'll follow you, look you pinion him, and take his money from him, lest he swallow a
shilling, and kill himself.

2ND INTELLIGENCER
Get thou on before.

[Exeunt.

SCÆNA SECUNDA

Enter the **DUKE**, the **COUNT**, **GONDARINO**, and **ARRIDO**.

DUKE
Now Gondarino, what can you put on now
That may again deceive us?
Have ye more strange illusions, yet more mists,
Through which, the weak eye may be led to error:
What can ye say that may do satisfaction
Both for her wrong'd honor, and your ill?

GONDARINO
All I can say, or may, is said already:
She is unchaste, or else I have no knowledge,
I do not breathe, nor have the use of sense.

DUKE
Dare ye be yet so wilful, ignorant of your own
nakedness? did not your servants
In mine own hearing confess
They brought her to that house we found her in,
Almost by force: and with a great distrust
Of some ensuing hazard?

COUNT
He that hath begun so worthily,
It fits not with his resolution
To leave off thus, my Lord, I know these are but idle proofs.
What says your Lordship to them?

GONDARINO

Count, I dare yet pronounce again, thy Sister is not honest.

COUNT

You are your self my Lord, I like your setledness.

GONDARINO

Count, thou art young, and unexperienc'd in the dark, hidden ways of Women: Thou dar'st affirm with confidence, a Lady of fifteen may be a Maid.

COUNT

Sir, if it were not so, I have a Sister would set near my heart.

GONDARINO

Let her sit near her shame, it better fits her: call back the bloud that made our stream in nearness, and turn the Current to a better use; 'tis too much mudded, I do grieve to know it.

DUKE

Dar'st thou make up again, dar'st thou turn face, knowing we know thee, hast thou not been discover'd openly? did not our ears hear her deny thy courtings? did we not see her blush with modest anger, to be so overtaken by a trick; can ye deny this Lord?

GONDARINO

Had not your Grace, and her kind brother
Been within level of her eye,
You should have had a hotter volley from her,
More full of bloud and fire, ready to leap the window where she stood.
So truly sensual is her appetite.

DUKE

Sir, Sir, these are but words and tricks, give me the proof.

COUNT

What need a better proof than your Lordship?
I am sure ye have lain with her my Lord.

GONDARINO

I have confest it Sir.

DUKE

I dare not give thee credit without witness.

GONDARINO

Does your grace think we carry seconds with us, to search us, and see fair play: your Grace hath been ill tutor'd in the business; but if you hope to try her truly, and satisfy your self what frailty is, give her the Test: do not remember Count she is your Sister; nor let my Lord the Duke believe she is fair; but put her to it without hope or pity, then ye shall see that golden form flie off, that all eyes wonder at for pure and fixt, and under't base blushing Copper; metall not worth the meanest honor: you shall behold her then my Lord transparent, look through her heart, and view the spirits how they leap, and tell me then I did belie the Lady.

DUKE
It shall be done: come Gondarino bear us company,
We do believe thee: she shall die, and thou shalt see it.

[Enter **LAZARELLO**, **TWO INTELLIGENCERS**, and **GUARD**.

How now my friends, whome have you guarded hither?

2ND INTELLIGENCER
So please your Grace we have discover'd a villain and a
Traitor: the Lord Lucio hath examin'd him, and sent him to your
Grace for Judgement.

COUNT
My Lord, I dare absolve him from all sin of Treason: I know his most ambition is but a dish of meat; which he hath hunted with so true a scent, that he deserveth the Collar not the Halter.

DUKE
Why do they bring him thus bound up? the poor man had more need of some warm meat, to comfort his cold stomach.

COUNT
Your Grace shall have the cause hereafter, when you may laugh more freely:
But these are call'd Informers: men that live by Treason, as
Rat-catchers do by poison.

DUKE
Would there were no heavier prodigies hung over us, than this poor fellow, I durst redeem all perils ready to pour themselves upon this State, with a cold Custard.

COUNT
Your Grace might do it without danger to your person.

LAZARELLO
My Lord, if ever I intended treason against your Person, or the State, unless it were by wishing from your Table some dish of meat, which I must needs confess, was not a subjects part: or coveting by stealth, sups from those noble bottles, that no mouth, keeping allegiance true, should dare to taste: I must confess, with more than covetous eye, I have beheld those dear conceal'd dishes, that have been brought in by cunning equipage, to wait upon your Graces pallat: I do confesse, out of this present heat, I have had Stratagems and Ambuscado's; but God be thank'd they have never took.

DUKE
Count, this business is your own; when you have done, repair to us.

[Exit **DUKE**.

COUNT

I will attend your Grace: Lazarello, you are at liberty, be your own man again; and if you can be master of your wishes, I wish it may be so.

LAZARELLO

I humbly thank your Lordship: I must be unmannerly, I have some present business, once more I heartily thank your Lordship.

[Exit **LAZARELLO**.

COUNT

Now even a word or two to you, and so farewell; you think you have deserv'd much of this State by this discovery: y'are a slavish people, grown subject to the common course of all men. How much unhappy were that noble spirit, could work by such baser gains? what misery would not a knowing man put on with willingness, e'r he see himself grown fat and full fed, by fall of those you rise by? I do discharge ye my attendance; our healthful State needs no such Leeches to suck out her bloud.

1ST INTELLIGENCER

I do beseech your Lordship.

2ND INTELLIGENCER

Good my Lord.

COUNT

Go learn to be more honest, when I see you work your means from honest industry,

[Exeunt **INTELLIGENCERS**.

I will be willing to accept your labours:
Till then I will keep back my promis'd favours:
Here comes another remnant of folly:

[Enter **LUCIO**.

I must dispatch him too. Now Lord Lucio, what business bring you hither?

LUCIO

Faith Sir, I am discovering what will become of that notable piece of treason, intended by that Varlet Lazarillo; I have sent him to the Duke for judgement.

COUNT

Sir, you have perform'd the part of a most careful Statesman, and let me say it to your face, Sir, of a Father to this State: I would wish you to retire, and insconce your self in study: for such is your daily labour, and our fear, that our loss of an hour may breed our overthrow.

LUCIO

Sir, I will be commanded by your judgement, and though I find it a trouble scant to be waded through, by these weak years: yet for the dear care of the Commonwealth, I will bruise my brains, and confine my self to much vexation.

COUNT
Go, and maist thou knock down Treason like an Ox.

LUCIO
Amen.

[Exeunt.

[Enter **MERCER, PANDAR, FRANCISSINA**.

MERCER
Have I spoke thus much in the honor of Learning? learn'd the names of the seven liberal Sciences, before my marriage; and since, have in haste written Epistles congratulatory, to the Nine Muses, and is she prov'd a Whore and a Begger?

PANDAR
'Tis true, you are not now to be taught, that no man can be learn'd of a suddain; let not your first project discourage you, what you have lost in this, you may get again in Alchumie.

FRANCISSINA
Fear not Husband, I hope to make as good a wife, as the best of your neighbors have, and as honest.

MERCER
I will goe home; good Sir, do not publish this, as long as it runs amongst our selves; 'tis good honest mirth: you'll come home to supper; I mean to have all her friends, and mine, as ill as it goes.

PANDAR
Do wisely Sir, and bid your own friends, your whole wealth will scarce feast all hers, neither is it for your credit, to walk the streets with a woman so noted; get you home and provide her cloaths: let her come an hour hence with an Hand-basket, and shift her self, she'll serve to sit at the upper end of the Table, and drink to your customers.

MERCER
Art is just, and will make me amends.

PANDAR
No doubt Sir.

MERCER
The chief note of a Scholar you say, is to govern his passions; wherefore I do take all patiently; in sign of which, my most dear Wife, I do kiss thee, make haste home after me, I shall be in my study.

[Exit **MERCER**.

PANDAR
Go, avaunt, my new City Dame, send me what you promis'd me for consideration; and may'st thou prove a Lady.

FRANCISSINA
Thou shalt have it, his Silks shall flie for it.

[Exeunt.

[Enter **LAZARELLO** and his **BOY**.

LAZARELLO
How sweet is a Calm after a Tempest, what is there now that can stand betwixt me and felicity? I have gone through all my crosses constantly; have confounded my enemies, and know where to have my longings satisfied: I have my way before me, there's the door, and I may freely walk into my delights: knock boy.

JULIA [Within]
Who's there?

LAZARELLO
Madona, my Love, not guilty, not guilty, open the door.

[Enter **JULIA**.

JULIA
Art thou come sweet-heart?

LAZARELLO
Yes, to thy soft embraces, and the rest of my over-flowing blisses; come, let us in and swim in our delights: a short Grace as we go, and so to meat.

JULIA
Nay my dear Love, you must bear with me in this; we'll to the Church first.

LAZARELLO
Shall I be sure of it then?

JULIA
By my love you shall.

LAZARELLO
I am content, for I do now wish to hold off longer, to whet my appetite, and do desire to meet with more troubles, so I might conquer them:
And as a holy Lover that hath spent
The tedious night with many a sigh and tears;
Whilst he pursu'd his wench: and hath observ'd
The smiles, and frowns, not daring to displease

When at last, hath with his service won
Her yielding heart; that she begins to dote
Upon him, and can hold no longer out,
But hangs about his neck, and wooes him more
Than ever he desir'd her love before:
Then begins to flatter his desert,
And growing wanton, needs will cast her off;
Try her, pick quarrels, to breed fresh delight,
And to increase his pleasing appetite.

JULIA
Come Mouse will you walk?

LAZARELLO
I pray thee let me be deliver'd of the joy I am so big with, I do feel that high heat within me, that I begin to doubt whether I be mortal:
How I contemn my fellows in the Court,
With whom I did but yesterday converse?
And in a lower, and an humbler key
Did walk and meditate on grosser meats?
There are they still poor rogues, shaking their chops,
And sneaking after Cheeses, and do run
Headlong in chace, of every Jack of Beer
That crosseth them, in hope of some repast,
That it will bring them to, whilst I am here,
The happiest wight that ever set his tooth
To a dear novelty: approach my love,
Come, let's go to knit the True Loves knot,
That never can be broken.

BOY
That is to marry a whore.

LAZARELLO
When that is done, then will we taste the gift,
Which Fates have sent my Fortunes up to lift.

BOY
When that is done, you'll begin to repent upon a full stomach; but I see, 'tis but a form in destiny, not to be alter'd.

[Exeunt.

[Enter **ARRIGO** and **ORIANA**.

ORIANA
Sir, what may be the current of your business, that thus you single out your time and place?

ARRIGO
Madam, the business now impos'd upon me, concerns you nearly, I wish some worser man might finish it.

ORIANA
Why are ye chang'd so? are ye not well Sir?

ARRIGO
Yes Madam, I am well, wo'd you were so.

ORIANA
Why Sir, I feel my self in perfect health.

ARRIGO
And yet ye cannot live long, Madam.

ORIANA
Why good Arrigo?

ARRIGO
Why? ye must dye.

ORIANA
I know I must, but yet my fate calls not upon me.

ARRIGO
It does; this hand the Duke commands shall give you death.

ORIANA
Heaven, and the powers Divine, guard well the innocent.

ARRIGO
Lady, your Prayers may do your soul some good,
That sure your body cannot merit by 'em:
You must prepare to die.

ORIANA
What's my offence? what have these years committed,
That may be dangerous to the Duke, or State?
Have I conspir'd by poison, have I giv'n up
My honor to some loose unsetl'd bloud
That may give action to my plots?
Dear Sir, let me not dye ignorant of my faults?

ARRIGO
Ye shall not.
Then Lady, you must know, you're held unhonest;
The Duke, your Brother, and your friends in Court,

With too much grief condemn ye: though to me,
The fault deserves not to be paid with death.

ORIANA
Who's my accuser?

ARRIGO
Lord Gondarino.

ORIANA
Arrigo, take these words, and bear them to the Duke,
It is the last petition I shall ask thee:
Tell him the child this present hour brought forth
To see the world has not a soul more pure, more white,
More Virgin than I have; Tell him Lord Gondarino's Plot, I suffer for, and willingly: tell him it had been a
greater honor, to have sav'd than kill'd: but I have done: strike, I am arm'd for heaven. Why, stay you? is
there any hope?

ARRIGO
I would not strike.

ORIANA
Have you the power to save?

ARRIGO
With hazard of my life, if it should be known.

ORIANA
You will not venture that?

ARRIGO
I will Lady: there is that means yet to escape your death, if you can wisely apprehend it.

ORIANA
Ye dare not be so kind?

ARRIGO
I dare, and will, if you dare but deserve't.

ORIANA
If I should slight my life, I were to blame.

ARRIGO
Then Madam, this is the means, or else you die: I love you.

ORIANA
I shall believe it, if you save my life.

ARRIGO
And you must lie with me.

ORIANA
I dare not buy my life so.

ARRIGO
Come, ye must resolve, say yea or no.

ORIANA
Then no; nay, look not ruggedly upon me, I am made up too strong to fear such looks: Come, do your Butchers part: before I would wish life, with the dear loss of honour, I dare find means to free my self.

ARRIGO
Speak, will ye yield?

ORIANA
Villain, I will not; Murtherer, do thy worst, thy base unnoble thoughts dare prompt thee to; I am above thee slave.

ARRIGO
Wilt thou not be drawn to yield by fair perswasions?

ORIANA
No, nor by—

ARRIGO
Peace, know your doom then; your Ladyship must remember, you are not now at home, where you dare jeast at all that come about you: but you are fallen under my mercy, which shall be but small; if thou refuse to yield: hear what I have sworn unto myself; I will enjoy thee, though it be between the parting of thy soul and body; yield yet and live.

ORIANA
I'll guard the one, let Heaven guard the other.

ARRIGO
Are you so resolute then?

DUKE [from above]
Hold, hold I say.

ORIANA
What have I? yet more terror to my tragedy?

ARRIGO
Lady, the Scene of bloud is done; ye are now as free from scandal, as from death.

[Enter **DUKE**, **COUNT**, and **GONDARINO**.

DUKE

Thou Woman which wert born to teach men virtue,
Fair, sweet, and modest Maid, forgive my thoughts,
My trespass was my love.
Seize Gondarino, let him wait our dooms.

GONDARINO

I do begin a little to love this woman; I could endure her already twelve miles off.

COUNT

Sister, I am glad you have brought your honor off so fairly, without loss: you have done a work above your sex, the Duke admires it: give him fair encounter.

DUKE

Best of all comforts, may I take this hand, and call it
mine?

ORIANA

I am your Graces handmaid.

DUKE

Would ye had sed my self: might it not be so Lady?

COUNT

Sister, say I, I know you can afford it.

ORIANA

My Lord, I am your subject, you may command me, provided still, your thoughts be fair and good.

DUKE

Here I am yours, and when I cease to be so,
Let heaven forget me: thus I make it good.

ORIANA

My Lord, I am no more mine own.

COUNT

So, this bargain was well driven.

GONDARINO

Duke, thou hast sold away thy self to all perdition; thou art this present hour becomming Cuckold: methinks I see thy gaul grate through thy veins, and jealousie seize thee with her talons: I know that womans nose must be cut off, she cannot scape it.

DUKE

Sir, we have punishment for you.

ORIANA

I do beseech your Lordship, for the wrongs this man hath done me, let me pronounce his punishment.

DUKE

Lady, I give't to you, he is your own.

GONDARINO

I do beseech your Grace, let me be banisht with all the speed that may be.

COUNT

Stay still, you shall attend her sentence.

ORIANA

Lord Gondarino, you have wrong'd me highly; yet since it sprung from no peculiar hate to me, but from a general dislike unto all women, you shall thus suffer for it; Arrigo, call in some Ladies to assist us; will your Grace take your State?

GONDARINO

My Lord, I do beseech your Grace for any punishment saving this woman, let me be sent upon discovery of some Island; I do desire but a small Gondela, with ten Holland Cheeses, and I'll undertake it.

ORIANA

Sir, ye must be content, will ye sit down? nay, do it willingly: Arrigo, tie his Arms close to the chair, I dare not trust his patience.

GONDARINO

Mayst thou be quickly old and painted; mayst thou dote upon some sturdy Yeoman of the Wood-yard, and he be honest; mayst thou be barr'd the lawful lechery of thy Coach, for want of instruments; and last, be thy womb unopen'd.

DUKE

This fellow hath a pretty gaul.

COUNT

My Lord, I hope to see him purg'd e'r he part.

[Enter **LADIES**.

ORIANA

Your Ladyships are welcome: I must desire your helps, though you are no Physitians, to do a strange cure upon this Gentleman.

LADIES

In what we can assist you Madam, ye may command us.

GONDARINO

Now do I sit like a Conjurer within my circle, and these the Devils that are rais'd about me, I will pray that they may have no power upon me.

ORIANA
Ladies, fall off in couples, then with a soft still march, with low demeanors, charge this Gentleman, I'll be your Leader.

GONDARINO
Let me be quarter'd Duke quickly, I can endure it: these women long for Mans flesh, let them have it.

DUKE
Count, have you ever seen so strange a passion? what would this fellow do, if he should find himself in bed with a young Lady?

COUNT
'Faith my Lord, if he could get a knife, sure he wou'd cut her throat, or else he wou'd do as Hercules did by Lycas, swing out her soul: h'as the true hate of a woman in him.

ORIANA
Low with your Cursies Ladies.

GONDARINO
Come not too near me, I have a breath will poison ye, my lungs are rotten, and my stomach is raw: I am given much to belching: hold off, as you love sweet airs; Ladies, by your first nights pleasure, I conjure you, as you wou'd have your Husbands proper men, strong backs, and little legs, as you would have 'em hate your Waiting-women.

ORIANA
Sir, we must court ye, till we have obtain'd some little favour from those gracious eyes, 'tis but a kiss a piece.

GONDARINO
I pronounce perdition to ye all; ye are a parcel of that damned crew that fell down with Lucifer, and here ye staid on earth to plague poor men; vanish, avaunt, I am fortified against your charms; heaven grant me breath and patience.

1ST LADY
Shall we not kiss then?

GONDARINO
No sear my lips with hot irons first, or stitch them up like a Ferrets: oh that this brunt were over!

2ND LADY
Come, come, little rogue, thou art too maidenly by my troth, I think I must box thee till thou be'st bolder; the more bold, the more welcome: I prethee kiss me, be not afraid.

[She sits on his knee.

GONDARINO

If there be any here, that yet have so much of the fool left in them, as to love their mothers, let them looke on her, and loath them too.

2ND LADY

What a slovenly little villain art thou, why dost thou not stroke up thy hair? I think thou ne'er comb'st it: I must have it lie in better order; so, so, so, let me see thy hands, are they wash'd?

GONDARINO

I would they were loose for thy sake.

DUKE

She tortures him admirably.

COUNT

The best that ever was.

2ND LADY

Alas, how cold they are, poor golls, why dost thee not get thee a Muff?

ARRIGO

Madam, here's an old Countrey Gentlewoman at the door, that came nodding up for justice, she was with the Lord Gondarino to day, and would now again come to the speech of him, she says.

ORIANA

Let her in, for sports sake, let her in.

GONDARINO

Mercy, oh Duke, I do appeal to thee: plant Canons there, and discharge them against my breast rather: nay, first let this she-fury sit still where she does, and with her nimble fingers stroke my hair, play with my fingers ends, or any thing, until my panting heart have broke my breast.

DUKE

You must abide her censure. The Lady rises from his knee.

[Enter old **GENTLEWOMAN**.

GONDARINO

I see her come, unbutton me, for she will speak.

GENTLEWOMAN

Where is he Sir?

GONDARINO

Save me, I hear her.

ARRIGO

There he is in state to give you audience.

GENTLEWOMAN
How does your good Lordship?

GONDARINO
Sick of the spleen.

GENTLEWOMAN
How?

GONDARINO
Sick.

GENTLEWOMAN
Will you chew a Nutmeg, you shall not refuse it, it is very comfortable.

GONDARINO
Nay, now thou art come, I know it
Is the Devils Jubile, Hell is broke loose:
My Lord, if ever I have done you service,
Or have deserv'd a favour of your Grace,
Let me be turn'd upon some present action,
Where I may sooner die, than languish thus;
Your Grace hath her petition, grant it her, and ease me now at last.

DUKE
No Sir, you must endure.

GENTLEWOMAN
For my petition, I hope your Lordship hath remembred me.

ORIANA
'Faith I begin to pity him, Arrigo, take her off, bear her away, say her petition is granted.

GENTLEWOMAN
Whither do you draw me Sir? I know it is not my Lords pleasure I should be thus used, before my business be dispatched?

ARRIGO
You shall know more of that without.

ORIANA
Unbind him Ladies, but before he go, this he shall promise; for the love I bear to our own sex, I would have them still hated by thee, and injoyn thee as a punishment, never hereafter willingly to come in the presence, or sight of any woman, nor never to seek wrongfully the publick disgrace of any.

GONDARINO

'Tis that I would have sworn, and do: when I meddle with them, for their good, or their bad; may Time call back this day again, and when I come in their companies, may I catch the pox, by their breath, and have no other pleasure for it.

DUKE
Ye are too merciful.

ORIANA
My Lord, I shew'd my sex the better.

GONDARINO
All is over-blown Sister: y'are like to have a fair night of it, and a Prince in your Arms: let's goe my Lord.

DUKE
Thus through the doubtful streams of joy and grief, True
Love doth wade, and finds at last relief.

[Exeunt **OMNES**.

EPILOGUE (At a Revival)
The monuments of virtue and desert
Appear more goodly when the gloss of art
Is eaten off by time, than when at first
They were set up, not censured at the worst:
We have done our best, for your contents, to fit,
With new pains, this old monument of wit.

Francis Beaumont – A Short Biography

Francis Beaumont was born in 1584 near the small Leicestershire village of Thringstone. Unfortunately precise records of much of his short life do not exist.

He was the son to Sir Francis Beaumont of Grace Dieu, a justice of the common pleas. His mother was Anne, the daughter of Sir George Pierrepont.

The first date we can give for his education is at age 13 when he begins at Broadgates Hall (now Pembroke College, Oxford). Sadly, his father died the following year, 1598. Beaumont left university without a degree and entered the Inner Temple in London in 1600. A career choice of Law taken previously by his father.

The information to hand is confident that Beaumont's career in law was short-lived. He was quickly attracted to the theatre and soon became first an admirer and then a student of poet and playwright Ben Jonson. Jonson at this time was a cultural behemoth; very talented and a life full of volatility that included frequent brushes with the authorities. His followers, including the poet Robert Herrick, were known as 'the sons of Ben'. Beaumont was also on friendly terms with other luminaries such as the poet Michael Drayton.

Beaumont's first work was Salmacis and Hermaphroditus, it debuted in 1602. A 1911 edition of the Encyclopædia Britannica includes the description "not on the whole discreditable to a lad of eighteen, fresh from the popular love-poems of Marlowe and Shakespeare, which it naturally exceeds in long-winded and fantastic diffusion of episodes and conceits."

By 1605, Beaumont had written commendatory verses to Volpone one of Ben Jonson's masterpieces.

It was now, in the early years of the 17th Century, that he met John Fletcher and together they gradually formed one of the most dynamic and productive of writing teams that English theatre has ever produced.

Their playwriting careers at this stage were both troubled by early failure. Beaumont had written The Knight of the Burning Pestle and it was first performed by the Children of the Blackfriars company in 1607. The audience however was distinctly unimpressed. The publisher's epistle in the 1613 quarto says they failed to note "the privie mark of irony about it."

The following year, Fletcher's Faithful Shepherdess failed on the same stage.

In 1609, however, the two collaborated in earnest on Philaster. The play was performed by the King's Men at the Globe Theatre and at Blackfriars. It was a great success. Their careers were now well and truly launched and into the bargain they had ignited and captured a public taste for tragicomedy.

There is an account that at the time the two men shared everything. They lived together in a house on the Bankside in Southwark, " they also lived together in Bankside, sharing clothes and having "one wench in the house between them." Or as another account puts it "sharing everything in the closest intimacy."

This arrangement stopped in about 1613 when Beaumont married Ursula Isley, daughter and co-heiress of Henry Isley of Sundridge in Kent, by whom he had two daughters (one of them was born after his death).

Beaumont, at a very young age even for those times, was struck down by a stroke at some point in mid-1613, after which he was unable to write any more plays, but he did manage to write an elegy for Lady Penelope Clifton, who had died on 26th October 1613.

Francis Beaumont died on March 6th, 1616 and was buried in Westminster Abbey.

In his short life his canon was small but influential. Although he is seen more as a dramatist his poetry was celebrated even then and it continues to gain an avid readership to this day.

It was said at one point of the collaboration of Beaumont and Fletcher that "in their joint plays their talents are so ... completely merged into one, that the hand of Beaumont cannot clearly be distinguished from that of Fletcher." Whilst it was the view then it has not endured into modern times. Indeed, slowly but with certainty the name of Beaumont has been removed from many of their joint works. It has given way to other such luminaries as Philip Massinger, Nathan field and James Shirley.

John Fletcher was born in December, 1579 in Rye, Sussex. He was baptised on December 20th.

As can be imagined details of much of his life and career have not survived and, accordingly, only a very brief indication of his life and works can be given.

His father, Richard Fletcher, was a successful and rather ambitious cleric. From being the Dean of Peterborough he moved on to become the Bishop of Bristol, Bishop of Worcester and finally, shortly before his death, the Bishop of London. He was also the chaplain to Queen Elizabeth.

When he was Dean of Peterborough, Richard Fletcher, witnessed the execution of Mary, Queen of Scots. It was said he "knelt down on the scaffold steps and started to pray out loud and at length, in a prolonged and rhetorical style, as though determined to force his way into the pages of history". He cried out at her death, "So perish all the Queen's enemies!" All very dramatic but the family did have strong links to the Arts.

Young Fletcher appears at the very young age of eleven to have entered Corpus Christi College at Cambridge University in 1591. There are no records that he ever took a degree but there is some small evidence that he was being prepared for a career in the church.

However, what is clear is that this was soon abandoned as he joined the stream of people who would leave University and decamp to the more bohemian life of commercial theatre in London.

Unfortunately, his father fell out with Queen Elizabeth but appears to have been on his way to rehabilitation before his death in 1596. At his death he was, however, mired in debt.

The upbringing of the now teenage Fletcher and his seven siblings now passed to his paternal uncle, the poet and minor official Giles Fletcher. Giles, who had the patronage of the Earl of Essex may have been a liability rather than an advantage to the young Fletcher. With Essex involved in the failed rebellion against Elizabeth Giles was also tainted by association.

By 1606 John Fletcher appears to have equipped himself with the talents to become a playwright. Initially this appears to have been for the Children of the Queen's Revels, then performing at the Blackfriars Theatre.

Commendatory verses by Richard Brome in the Beaumont and Fletcher 1647 folio place Fletcher in the company of Ben Jonson, although it is not known when this friendship began. Jonson, of course, was a leviathan of English Literature, so admired that many of his literary friends and colleagues were simply known as 'Sons of Ben'. Fletcher's frequent early collaborator, Francis Beaumont, was also a friend of Jonson's.

Fletcher's early career was marked by one significant failure; The Faithful Shepherdess, his adaptation of Giovanni Battista Guarini's Il Pastor Fido, which was performed by the Blackfriars Children in 1608. In the preface to the printed edition of his play, Fletcher explained the failure as due to his audience's faulty expectations. They expected a pastoral tragicomedy to feature dances, comedy, and murder, with the shepherds presented in conventional stereotypes – as Fletcher put it, wearing "gray cloaks, with curtailed dogs in strings." Fletcher's preface is however best known for its pithy definition of tragicomedy: "A tragicomedy is not so called in respect of mirth and killing, but in respect it wants [i.e., lacks] deaths, which is enough to make it no tragedy; yet brings some near it, which is enough to make it no comedy." A comedy, he went on to say, must be "a representation of familiar people." His preface is critical of drama that features characters whose action violates nature.

In that case, Fletcher appears to have been developing a new style faster than audiences could comprehend. By 1609, however, he had found his stride. With Beaumont, he wrote Philaster, which became a hit for the King's Men and began a profitable association between Fletcher and that company. Philaster appears also to have begun a trend for tragicomedy. Fletcher's influence has also been said to have inspired some features of Shakespeare's late romances, and certainly his influence on the tragicomic work of other playwrights is even more marked.

By the middle of the 1610s, Fletcher's plays had achieved a popularity that rivalled Shakespeare's and cemented the pre-eminence of the King's Men in Jacobean London. After Beaumont's retirement, necessitated by ill-health, and then his early death in 1616, Fletcher continued working, both singly and in collaboration, until his death in 1625. By that time, he had produced, or had been credited with, close to fifty plays. This body of work remained a major part of the King's Men's repertory until the closing of the theatres in 1642 due to the Civil War.

At the beginning of his career Fletcher's most important collaborator was Francis Beaumont. The two wrote together for close to a decade, first for the Children of the Queen's Revels, and then for the King's Men. According to an anecdote transmitted or invented by John Aubrey, they also lived together in Bankside, sharing clothes and having "one wench in the house between them." This domestic arrangement, if it existed, was ended by Beaumont's marriage in 1613, and their dramatic partnership ended after Beaumont fell ill, probably of a stroke, that same year.

At this point Fletcher had written many plays with Beaumont and several others on his own. He seems to have been regarded as quite a talent although it should be remembered that playwrights were required to be prolific, to easily work with other collaborators and to produce work of quality and commercial appeal very quickly.

The King's Men, run by Philip Henslowe, was the most prestigious of the theatre companies and Fletcher now had an increasingly close association with it.

Fletcher collaborated with Shakespeare on Henry VIII, The Two Noble Kinsmen, and the now lost Cardenio, which some scholars say was the basis for Lewis Theobald's play Double Falsehood. (Theobald is regarded as one of the best Shakespearean editors. Whether his play is based on Cardenio or on some other is not absolutely known although Theobald certainly promoted it as his revision of the lost Shakespeare/Fletcher play.)

A play that Fletcher also wrote by himself at this time, The Woman's Prize or the Tamer Tamed, is also regarded as a sequel to The Taming of the Shrew.

In 1616, with the death of Shakespeare, Fletcher now appears to have entered into an enhanced arrangement with the King's Men on very similar terms to Shakespeare's. Fletcher would now write exclusively for the King's Men until his own death almost a decade later.

As well as continuing his solo productions Fletcher was still collaborating with other playwrights, mainly Philip Massinger, who, in turn, would succeed him as the in-house playwright for the King's Men.

Fletcher's popularity continued throughout his life; indeed, during the winter of 1621, he had three of his plays performed at court. His mastery is most notable in two dramatic types; tragicomedy and the comedy of manners.

John Fletcher died in 1625, it is thought of bubonic plague which, at the time, was undergoing further outbreaks.

He seems to have been buried in what is now Southwark Cathedral, although a precise location is not known. There is much made of an anecdote that Fletcher and Massinger (who died in 1640) share the same grave but it is more likely that both are buried within a few yards of each other and that the stone markers in the floor have confused the issue. One is marked 'Edmond Shakespeare 1607' and the other 'John Fletcher 1625' refers to Shakespeare's younger brother and the playwright. The churchyards were, more often than not, completely over-crowded and breeding grounds for disease. Precise record keeping was not a practiced skill.

During the later Commonwealth, many of the playwright's best-known scenes were kept alive as drolls. These were brief performances, usually condensed into one or two scenes and with the addition of music or song to satisfy the taste for plays while the theatres were closed under the Puritans. At the re-opening of the theatres in 1660, the plays in the Fletcher canon, in original form or revised, were by far the most common productions on the English stage. The most frequently revived plays suggest the developing taste for comedies of manners. Among the tragedies, The Maid's Tragedy and, especially, Rollo Duke of Normandy held the stage. Four tragicomedies (A King and No King, The Humorous Lieutenant, Philaster, and The Island Princess) were popular, perhaps in part for their similarity to and foreshadowing of heroic drama. Four comedies (Rule a Wife And Have a Wife, The Chances, Beggars' Bush, and especially The Scornful Lady) were also stage mainstays.

Despite his popularity, and it appears he was held in higher regard than Shakespeare at this time, his works steadily lost ground to those of Shakespeare and to new productions from other playwrights.

Since then Fletcher has increasingly become a subject only for occasional revivals and for specialists. Fletcher and his collaborators have been the subject of important bibliographic and critical studies, but the plays have been revived only infrequently.

Due to the frequent collaborations between all manner of playwrights, and the revisions carried out in later years, having a settled list of authorship to any given set of plays can be problematic. The works of Fletcher and others of this period most definitely fall into this category. It is as well to take into account that during this period theatres were quite often closed either due to outbreaks of the plague or to the prevailing political and moral climate. Printers, anxious to provide materials that would sell, were not above changing a name or two to enhance sales.

Although Fletcher collaborated most often with Beaumont and Massinger, it is believed that Massinger revised many of the plays some time after their original production. Other collaborators including Nathan Field, William Shakespeare, William Rowley and others also can be seen distinctly in Fletchers' works. Many modern scholars point out that Fletcher had many particular mannerisms, but other playwrights would also duplicate these at times so allocating exact contributions of anyone to a play is somewhat of a detective case in many instances. However, from the original folio printings or licensing via the Master of the Revels (the statutory licensing authority to approve and censor plays as well a hand in publication and printing of theatrical materials) as well as contemporary notes a fairly precise bibliography of the works can be given with only a few plays lacking substantial authority and provenance.

Francis Beaumont & John Fletcher – A Concise Bibliography

This bibliography gives the most likely date of writing together with when published, revised or licensed by the Master or the Revels (This position within the royal household was originally for royal festivities, ie revels, and later to oversee stage censorship, until this function was transferred to the Lord Chamberlain in 1624).

Francis Beaumont – Solo Plays
The Knight of the Burning Pestle, comedy (performed 1607; printed 1613)
The Masque of the Inner Temple and Gray's Inn, masque (printed 1613)

John Fletcher - Solo Plays
The Faithful Shepherdess, pastoral (written 1608–9; printed 1609)
The Tragedy of Valentinian, tragedy (1610–14; 1647)
Monsieur Thomas, comedy (c. 1610–16; 1639)
The Woman's Prize, or The Tamer Tamed, comedy (c. 1611; 1647)
Bonduca, tragedy (1611–14; 1647)
The Chances, comedy (c. 1613–25; 1647)
Wit Without Money, comedy (c. 1614; 1639)
The Mad Lover, tragicomedy (acted 5 January 1617; 1647)
The Loyal Subject, tragicomedy (licensed 16 November 1618; revised 1633; 1647)
The Humorous Lieutenant, tragicomedy (c. 1619; 1647)
Women Pleased, tragicomedy (c. 1619–23; 1647)
The Island Princess, tragicomedy (c. 1620; 1647)
The Wild Goose Chase, comedy (c. 1621; 1652)
The Pilgrim, comedy (c. 1621; 1647)
A Wife for a Month, tragicomedy (licensed 27 May 1624; 1647)
Rule a Wife and Have a Wife, comedy (licensed 19 October 1624; 1640)

Francis Beaumont & John Fletcher
The Woman Hater, comedy (1606; 1607)
Cupid's Revenge, tragedy (c. 1607–12; 1615)
Philaster, or Love Lies a-Bleeding, tragicomedy (c. 1609; 1620)
The Maid's Tragedy, Tragedy (c. 1609; 1619)
A King and No King, tragicomedy (1611; 1619)

The Captain, comedy (c. 1609–12; 1647)
The Scornful Lady, comedy (c. 1613; 1616)
Love's Pilgrimage, tragicomedy (c. 1615–16; 1647)
The Noble Gentleman, comedy (c. 1613; licensed 3 February 1626; 1647)

Their Collaborations with Others

With Philip Massinger
Thierry & Theodoret, tragedy (c. 1607; 1621)
The Coxcomb, comedy (c. 1608–10; 1647)
Beggars' Bush, comedy (c. 1612–13; revised 1622; 1647)
Love's Cure, comedy (c. 1612–13; revised 1625; 1647)

John Fletcher with Philip Massinger
Sir John van Olden Barnavelt, tragedy (August 1619; MS)
The Little French Lawyer, comedy (c. 1619–23; 1647)
A Very Woman, tragicomedy (c. 1619–22; licensed 6 June 1634; 1655)
The Custom of the Country, comedy (c. 1619–23; 1647)
The Double Marriage, tragedy (c. 1619–23; 1647)
The False One, history (c. 1619–23; 1647)
The Prophetess, tragicomedy (licensed 14 May 1622; 1647)
The Sea Voyage, comedy (licensed 22 June 1622; 1647)
The Spanish Curate, comedy (licensed 24 October 1622; 1647)
The Lovers' Progress or The Wandering Lovers, tragicomedy (licensed 6 December 1623; rev 1634; 1647)
The Elder Brother, comedy (c. 1625; 1637)

John Fletcher with Philip Massinger & Nathan Field
The Honest Man's Fortune, tragicomedy (1613; 1647)
The Queen of Corinth, tragicomedy (c. 1616–18; 1647)
The Knight of Malta, tragicomedy (c. 1619; 1647)

John Fletcher with William Shakespeare
Henry VIII, history (c. 1613; 1623)
The Two Noble Kinsmen, tragicomedy (c. 1613; 1634)
Cardenio, tragicomedy (c. 1613)

John Fletcher with Thomas Middleton & William Rowley
Wit at Several Weapons, comedy (c. 1610–20; 1647)

John Fletcher with William Rowley
The Maid in the Mill (licensed 29 August 1623; 1647).

John Fletcher with Nathan Field
Four Plays, or Moral Representations, in One, morality (c. 1608–13; 1647)

John Fletcher with Philip Massinger, Ben Jonson and George Chapman
Rollo Duke of Normandy, or The Bloody Brother, tragedy (c. 1617; revised 1627–30; 1639)

John Fletcher with James Shirley
The Night Walker, or The Little Thief, comedy (c. 1611; 1640)
The Coronation c. 1635

Uncertain
The Nice Valour, or The Passionate Madman, comedy (c. 1615–25; 1647)
The Laws of Candy, tragicomedy (c. 1619–23; 1647)
The Fair Maid of the Inn, comedy (licensed 22 January 1626; 1647)
The Faithful Friends, tragicomedy (registered 29 June 1660; MS.)

The Nice Valour is possibly by Fletcher revised by Thomas Middleton;

The Fair Maid of the Inn is perhaps a play by Massinger, John Ford, and John Webster, either with or without Fletcher's involvement.

The Laws of Candy has been variously attributed to Fletcher and to John Ford.

The Night-Walker was a Fletcher original, with additions by Shirley for a 1639 production.

Even now there is not absolute certainty on several of the plays. The first Beaumont & Fletcher folio of 1647 contained 35 plays and the second folio of 1679 added a further 18. In total 53 plays.

The first folio included The Masque of the Inner Temple and Gray's Inn (1613), and the second The Knight of the Burning Pestle (1607), widely considered Beaumont's solo works, although the latter was in early editions attributed to both writers. Fletcher himself said that Beaumont was attributed co-authorship of many works that belonged solely to Fletcher or to other collaborators.

One play in the canon, Sir John Van Olden Barnavelt, existed in manuscript and was not published till 1883.

www.ingramcontent.com/pod-product-compliance
Lightning Source LLC
Chambersburg PA
CBHW060133050426
42448CB00010B/2095